ANGELS AND DEMONS

"The Angel Appearing to Joshua"
Illustration for Old Testament
GUSTAV DORÉ

PETER J. KREEFT

ANGELS AND DEMONS

What Do We Really Know about Them?

IGNATIUS PRESS SAN FRANCISCO

Cover art:
The Archangel Michael.
La Martorana, Palermo, Italy
Scala/Art Resource, New York
Cover design by Roxanne Mei Lum

ISBN 0–89870–550–9
Library of Congress catalogue number 95–76525
Printed in the United States of America

This book is dedicated to

Francis/ces and Frodo
my wife's and my guardian angels
who have been the real editors and ghost writers of this book
through their gentle inspirations
and their muted laughter

and to

Tranquillo (Tony) Massi
my father-in-law
who sat at the edge of his children's beds
lulling them to sleep
with stories of St. Michael the Archangel betting with Lucifer
and who is now most likely losing
a game of poker (as usual) to an angel

CONTENTS

Introduction 13

PART ONE: Questions about Our Fascination with Angels

1 *O.K., so I'm browsing through this book and wondering: why should I buy it? What can you tell me about angels in one page?* 17

2 *Why are there so many angel books around lately?* 18

3 *Why are angels fascinating?* 20

4 *What* difference *does it make whether you believe in angels or not?* 21

PART TWO: Questions about How We Know Anything about Angels

5 *Are you an expert on angels?* 27

6 *Then what gives you the authority to write a book on angels?* 27

7 *How do you know anything about angels? Isn't it all undisciplined guesswork and imagination?* 28

8 *Can you prove the reality of the supernatural?* 29

9 *Isn't the supernatural unscientific?* 32

10 *Are there any purely logical reasons for believing in angels apart from faith in the data in the Bible and people's stories of meeting angels?* 33

11 *Why can't there be a logical proof of the existence of angels?* 36

12 *Are angels* necessary? 37

13 *Why do people believe in angels?* 38

14 *Why do many people think it's stupid to believe in angels?* 39
15 *Why not believe in God without angels? Who needs angels?* 39
16 *What about the opposite: believing not in God without angels but in angels without God?* 41
17 *Can you be a Christian without believing in angels?* 42

PART THREE:: Questions about the Nature of Angels
18 *Of what are angels made?* 47
19 *How can angels be anything at all if they have no bodies? We can't imagine a spirit without a body.* 47
20 *Can you prove spirit exists? Can you prove materialism is untrue?* 48
21 *What is this "spirit" of which angels are made?* 50
22 *Are angels human souls without bodies? Are they the same as ghosts?* 50
23 *If angels have no bodies, how can we ever see them?* 52
24 *What have angels done in past history?* 53
25 *Do we become angels after we die?* 54
26 *Didn't Jesus say in the Bible (Matthew 22) that we would be "like the angels in heaven"?* 55
27 *If angels come from heaven, what is "heaven"?* 55
28 *Do angels have different personalities?* 56
29 *According to traditional angelology, angels are supposed to form a* hierarchy*. Why? Isn't this just a projection of medieval monarchical politics?* 58
30 *Hierarchy and inequality among angels sound unjust and unfair. Is God an elitist?* 59
31 *What's the most fascinating description of angels in literature? What do you most recommend that I read?* 60
32 *Are angels involved in politics?* 61
33 *Are angels comforting?* 62
34 *What do angels do all day? Don't they get bored?* 63
35 *How do angels "just have insights"?* 65

36 *How do angels communicate with each other?* 65
37 *How do angels communicate with God?* 67
38 *How do angels communicate with us?* 67
39 Where *are angels? Where do they live?* 68
40 *How do angels move?* 69
41 *How many angels can dance on the head of a pin?* 70
42 *What do angels really look like?* 71
43 *Are angels beautiful?* 72
44 *Do angels have a sense of humor?* 73
45 *Why did the medievals arrange angels into nine levels, or "choirs"?* 74
46 *Are there female angels?* 76
47 *Why do women see angels more often than men do?* 80
48 *Why are all the paintings of angels somehow unsuccessful?* 80
49 *Could angels be extraterrestrials?* 81
50 *Were the many gods worshipped by all ancient peoples (except the Jews) really angels?* 82
51 *How do you know if you are seeing an angel?* 83
52 *Are you sure angels have no wings? Why are they always painted with wings?* 83
53 *Why are angels painted with halos?* 83
54 *Do angels have a special connection with the sea?* 85
55 *Are angels especially connected with the stars?* 86
56 *Do angels love? If not, how can they be good without loving? If so, how can they have emotions without having bodies or nerves?* 88
57 *How many angels are there?* 91
58 *Do angels have sex?* 91
59 *Are angels eternal?* 92
60 *Do we each have a guardian angel? Are our guardian angels aware of us right now?* 93
61 *Do angels see God and us at the same time?* 93
62 *Can angels make us good?* 94

63 *Can reading books about angels and* thinking *about angels make us good?* 94
64 *Do angels know our secret thoughts?* 95
65 *How do angels affect our minds?* 96
66 *Can angels go through doors and walls?* 97
67 *How do angels act on bodies, if angels are bodiless spirits?* 97
68 *Can angels cheer us up and make us happy?* 98
69 *What are the different ways angels can affect us?* 100
70 *Do angels know the future?* 100
71 *Do angels ever raise or calm storms?* 101
72 *Can angels become cars?* 101
73 *Do angels eat?* 101
74 *Are the stories about rescues by angels true?* 102
75 *Can I expect ever to be rescued by an angel?* 102
76 *What do other religions say about angels?* 103
77 *Can we talk to angels?* 104
78 *Aren't angels irrelevant today? This is the age of man, isn't it?* 104
79 *Are there ever "angels in the outfield"? Do angels ever account for the outcome of baseball games?* 105
80 *Does each of us have his own angel?* 105
81 *What difference do guardian angels make?* 106
82 *When do our guardian angels come to us to fight for us?* 106
83 *Is the traditional picture of an angel whispering in one ear and a demon in the other true?* 106

PART FOUR: Questions about Demons
84 *Do demons, or devils, or evil spirits really exist?* 111
85 *Isn't it psychologically unhealthy to believe in demons? Isn't this a regression to medieval fear, superstition, and witch-hunting?* 112
86 *What difference does belief in demons make?* 113
87 *What can demons do?* 114

88 *Should we fear the devil and demon possession?* 114
89 *How did angels fall and become demons?* 116
90 *When did the angelic fall happen?* 119
91 *Explain the motivation for Satan's fall. Why would a wholly good angel choose to become a devil?* 120
92 *How do demons tempt us?* 120
93 *What are some specific ways devils tempt and deceive us, especially today? Please give me some detailed, specific, practical advice.* 122
94 *Is exorcism for real? Do exorcists really cast out demons?* 122
95 *Can demons possess cats? What about computers?* 123
96 *Could the false gods or idols that ancient peoples worshipped have been demons?* 123
97 *Is all "spiritual warfare" supernatural? Are demons our only enemies?* 124
98 *What can I do to help fight this spiritual war?* 125
99 *How can we mere men get supernatural help to fight supernatural foes? How should we pray?* 125
100 *Can angels help us to win this war?* 127

APPENDIX A: A Short Course in Angelistic Philosophy 129

APPENDIX B: A Snakebite Letter: Sex and the Media 136

APPENDIX C: What the New *Catechism of the Catholic Church* Says about Angels 145

APPENDIX D: Angels and Demons in the Bible 149

Bibliography 155

Art Credits 157

INTRODUCTION

This book has four parents.

The book's mother and its most immediate source, the womb from which it actually emerged, is the questions many people ask me about angels once they hear I'm writing a book about them and teaching a course about them. The book's agenda is the readers' questions, not the writer's.

The book's father was my unhappiness about the quality of angel books currently flooding the market and my surprised happiness about their quantity. There is a huge hunger out there, but it's being fed with fast food.

The book's godfather was a course I taught at Boston College called "Angels, Devils, Ghosts, and Miracles". It attracted not only many students but also many media inquiries.

The book's godmother was the absolutely fascinated sudden silence I have elicited from my classes every time I have mentioned the subject of angels and demons.

PART ONE

QUESTIONS ABOUT OUR FASCINATION WITH ANGELS

"The Death of St. Louis"
Illustration for Michaud's *History of the Crusades*
GUSTAV DORÉ

I *O.K., so I'm browsing through this book and wondering: why should I buy it? What can you tell me about angels in one page?*

1. They really exist. Not just in our minds, or our myths, or our symbols, or our culture. They are as real as your dog, or your sister, or electricity.

2. They're present, right here, right now, right next to you, reading these words with you.

3. They're not cute, cuddly, comfortable, chummy, or "cool". They are fearsome and formidable. They are huge. They are warriors.

4. They are the real "extra-terrestrials", the real "Supermen", the ultimate aliens. Their powers are far beyond those of all fictional creatures.

5. They are more brilliant minds than Einstein.

6. They can literally move the heavens and the earth if God permits them.

7. There are also evil angels, fallen angels, demons, or devils. These too are not myths. Demon possessions, and exorcisms, are real.

8. Angels are aware of you, even though you can't usually see or hear them. But you can communicate with them. You can talk to them without even speaking.

9. You really do have your very own "guardian angel". Everybody does.

10. Angels often come disguised. "Do not neglect hospitality, for some have entertained angels unawares"—that's a warning from life's oldest and best instruction manual.

11. We are on a protected part of a great battlefield between angels and devils, extending to eternity.

12. Angels are sentinels standing at the crossroads where life meets death. They work especially at moments of crisis, at the brink of disaster—for bodies, for souls, and for nations.

I think this is a far more serious and significant sign than most people realize. I think it's a symptom of fundamental changes that are happening, or about to happen, to our world. (In the Bible, angels usually appear just before world-changing and life-changing events.)

The explanation usually given is psychological and sociological.

The psychological part of this standard explanation of angels' newfound popularity is the *need for comfort* in a hard and increasingly violent, scary world.

The sociological part of the explanation is the changes in our culture that allow people to believe in angels again: the change from "modernism" to "postmodernism"—which means essentially the change from rationalism and faith in science to faith in something else: the irrational, or the occult, or the mystical, or just "something else". Angels fit into the category of "something else".

This standard explanation forgets something crucial.

In all the "expert" explanations of the "angel phenomenon", what answer is *never* given? An answer about what is objectively true! The psychological explanation talks about only what is subjectively "true for you": your need for comfort or security. The sociological explanation talks about only what's subjectively "true for a society": changing opinions, trends, fashions. What's forgotten is that angels are really there; that's the ultimate reason why people believe in them!

"I believe because . . ." "Because" is ambiguous. It could mean only a *subjective motive* ("Because I'm paranoid, I believe that man is going to kill me"), or it could mean an *objective reason* ("Because he's pointing a gun at me and squeezing the trigger, I believe that man is going to kill me"). "We believe in angels because we seek security" is only a subjective, psychological motive. "We believe in angels because God has revealed to us in the Bible that they exist" is an objective reason (though it's a reason that depends on faith, not on logical proof).

There are both good and bad subjective motives; and both good and bad objective reasons. Perhaps the need for security is a good subjective motive (I do not think it is), and perhaps the faith that the Bible is God's word is a bad objective reason (I do not think it is). But my point is simply that psychological motives are inadequate. The only honest reason for anyone ever to believe anything is that it is true, that it is really there. The same goes for angels too.

What about the sociological reason? Maybe the changes in our society are objective too, not just subjective. Maybe angels are really appearing more often now, and that's why there are more stories of people seeing them and more interest in them. Why do the sociologists and journalists never consider that simple explanation?

Why would they be appearing more now? That is one of the distinctive themes of this book. Angels appear on the brink of chaos, or catastrophe, or at least at the threat of chaos or catastrophe. They are spiritual soldiers in the great cosmic *jihad*, the spiritual war between Good and Evil.

That war seems to be coming to a head or making a fundamental turn right now, exactly at the time when most of our religious teachers have stopped talking about this fundamental biblical theme for the first time in thousands of years. Just when the enemy is making a great counterattack, we start forgetting we're on a battlefield at all!

Perhaps the angels are there to remind us, like soldiers in uniform.

3 *Why are angels fascinating?*

The first reason angels are fascinating is their *otherness*. They're utterly different from anything we ordinarily experience. They're fascinating for the same reason UFOs and extraterrestrial beings would be fascinating if they were real: they don't fit familiar earthly categories.

How fascinated would you be if aliens really landed here, if you knew it was not just a science fiction story but literal fact? Well, it is fact. Angels are the real aliens among us, the real extraterrestrials. They overcome the safe separation between the "out there" and the "down here". Meeting an angel is a true "close encounter" with an alien.

Second, we are naturally fascinated by intelligence in nonhuman form. That's why we also find the higher, more intelligent animals fascinating and why little children naturally love stories about talking animals. We can't stand being alone in the universe.

I once gave a questionnaire to a few hundred of my college students and asked, among other strange questions, these two: (1) Are you very interested in angels? (2) Are you very interested in animals? I expected that these two questions would divide the students into the "materialists", who would be interested in animals but not angels, and the "spiritualists", who would be interested in angels but not animals. But I found instead that most students were interested either in both animals and angels or in neither. Those who were interested in neither were usually majoring in, and thus interested in, sociology, politics, or economics. The abstractions of ideology and finance are much more mundane than the smell of a dog. There may be dogs in heaven (why not?), but not dollars.

A third reason we are fascinated with angels is that they are really superior beings. We are supposed to think that superiority is somehow suspicious and that equality is good and true and even beautiful. But deep down we know that equality is boring and that superiority and hierarchy and excellence are true *and* good *and* (especially) beautiful. We secretly long to bend the knee. Angels don't fit into our flat, one-level, ranch-style modern universe. They fit the old vertical universe. They're superior; they're supernatural.

4 *What* difference *does it make whether you believe in angels or not?*

That's a good question. Even though the objective question comes first—Do angels really exist?—the subjective question is important too—If they exist, why are they important for me and my life? What difference does it make to me whether I believe in angels or not?

Wait. First, what does the question mean? "Believing in" can mean three different things:

1. It can mean simply *an opinion*, like believing it will rain tomorrow.
2. It can mean *personal trust* or reliance, like believing in your doctor.
3. Or it can mean *religious faith, saving faith*, giving your whole heart and self and life to God in adoration and submission.

Believing in angels in the first sense makes only a mental difference in your map of the universe.

Believing in angels in the second sense makes a real and important difference to your life. It means you trust angels to guard you.

Believing in angels in the third sense is idolatry, worshipping false gods.

Clearly we are talking about belief in the first and second senses.

Back to our question: What difference does it make to believe in angels?

1. Even belief in the first, weakest sense—a mental opinion—makes two important psychological differences. First, it opens your mind. It overcomes materialism. It stretches your spirit beyond your senses and your mundane world. It gives your spiritual muscles exercise. Your feet are supposed to be on the ground, like tree roots, but your spirit is supposed to be in the heavens, like tree branches.

2. Second, it feeds the feeling of wonder, fascination, curiosity. It gives you the feeling of a small child in a large house with many rooms and stories and mysteries in it. It is an antidote to the poisonous modern feeling of being in a small, stuffy, boring, polluted, trivial, one-level universe.

3. If the belief is not just mental opinion but personal trust, it also gives you another feeling you had as a child: the feeling of holding the hand of a very big, strong person who guards and guides you. A feeling of security and hope.

4. Belief in angels makes an even bigger difference if you believe in God and pray, because your prayers to God to send angel help will be answered. They will make a difference to your life, for even though you can't see or hear your guardian angel, he can see and hear you. (See questions 60 and 82 on guardian angels.) He can even know your thoughts if you will to reveal them to him (but not if you don't: see question 64). You can talk to him by a kind of mental telepathy. You're not a telepath (probably), but he is.

If prayer doesn't really make a difference, if God is unmoved by our prayers, then it's a sham, like a friend saying, "I hear you. Don't worry. I'll take care of it"—and then doing nothing. Some people may be like that, but not God. Good people are not like that, and angels aren't either.

In fact, I strongly suspect that if we saw all the difference even the tiniest of our prayers to God make, and all the people those little prayers were destined to affect, and all the consequences of those effects down through the centuries, we would be so paralyzed with awe at the power of prayer that we would be unable to get up off our knees for the rest of our lives.

PART TWO

QUESTIONS ABOUT HOW WE KNOW ANYTHING ABOUT ANGELS

"Abraham's Sacrifice"
Psalter of Ingeburg of Denmark (13th cent.)
Musée Condé, Chantilly, France

5 *Are you an expert on angels?*

No. I'm not an expert on anything. There *are* no experts on angels, except angels, and I'm no angel.

6 *Then what gives you the authority to write a book on angels?*

I've piggybacked on a lot of giants who knew a lot more about angels than you or I do. As medieval philosophers loved to say, even dwarfs can see far if they have the good sense and humility to climb up onto the shoulders of giants—like Moses and Jesus and Augustine and Aquinas and saints and mystics. This book is not just me. It's 90 per cent unoriginal. That's what makes it different. Those tiresome and shallow modern books that all say the same thing are too desperately striving to be original. In every area of life the secret of originality is to stop trying to be original and just tell the truth as you see it.

Most of what I know about angels I learned from Saint Thomas Aquinas. Not all my answers are directly from him, but the principles from which I deduce my answers usually are. He was surely the greatest theologian of all time, and he happened to be also the one who wrote the most definitive treatise on angels, in the *Summa Theologica.* Each philosopher in the Middle Ages had a distinctive nickname, and Thomas' was the "Angelic Doctor". He was angelic in his *manner*—sublime, clear, unprejudiced, brilliant, rational, not driven by passions—as well as in his *matter*: the closest thing to an "expert" on angels.

7 *How do you know anything about angels? Isn't it all undisciplined guesswork and imagination?*

No, it isn't. Angelology is a *science*, though not an empirical science. It uses an essentially scientific method: gathering data and formulating theories to explain the data. The theories are controlled by the data.

Of course it's not laboratory data. Different sciences have different data. History, mathematics, and textual criticism are all sciences, but none of *them* have laboratory data either.

The data about angels come from two sources: the Bible and human experience (accounts of people meeting angels). Accepting the Bible as data requires faith, of course. But so does accepting *any* data! Accepting the thousands of published accounts (or millions of unpublished accounts) of people meeting angels also means faith: faith not in God but in humanity this time. It is a faith that should be critically questioned and evaluated, of course, but the beginning is faith. Accepting old documents as data is the historian's faith. (And this faith also should be critically questioned and evaluated.) Accepting a text as data to interpret is a kind of faith. Even believing in the validity of human reason and trusting the innate programming of the computers in our brains is faith—a faith that is presupposed in mathematics. After all, if an evil spirit or blind chance programmed our computers, why would we trust them? If our brains were not designed by God but by Satan or by no one, why should we trust them? Would you trust a computer programmed by randomly throwing marbles at its keyboard?

Angelology has data, and its theories are justified by its data. For instance, the traditional theory of angels, which I will try to explain and defend in this book, says that angels are (1) creatures of God, (2) bodiless spirits, (3) with intelligence (4) and will, (5) who live in God's presence in heaven, (6) obey his will, (7) carry his messages (*angel* means "messenger"), (8) assume bodies as we assume costumes, (9) influence our imagination (10) but not our free will, and (11) move material things supernaturally. If any one of the points in this theory were false, the data would be different. That is the justification for the theory. For instance, if angels could not assume bodies, they could not eat. However, in Scripture they do on occasion eat (see Gen 19:13); therefore they can assume bodies.

The only reason people today are much more suspicious of angelology than in any previous time or place or culture is naturalism, the philosophy that denies the supernatural. If the data about angels didn't claim anything miraculous or supernatural, it would be accepted just as data about other natural beings and events is accepted even if it is unusual (like platypuses in zoology or multiple personalities in psychology).

8 *Can you prove the reality of the supernatural?*

Even if I can't, you also can't prove its nonexistence. Naturalism cannot be proved. How could the fish in a little fishbowl prove that there is no world outside the fishbowl? How could an unborn baby prove there is no life outside the womb? How could man, bound to nature, prove there is nothing in addition to nature? You can't prove a universal negative—that there is no X anywhere (unless X is self-contradictory, like a round square)—for to prove there is no X anywhere, you would have to look everywhere. Only God can do that.

I think we *can* prove the reality of the supernatural, but we must first define *supernatural.*

Let's not define *supernatural* so narrowly that it means only the occult or the mystical—things you'd read about in the "metaphysics" sections of California bookstores. (That's a radical misunderstanding of the meaning of metaphysics, by the way; metaphysics means the philosophy of being, or thinking about the laws and principles that apply to everything, not just about the magical or even the supernatural.)

Let's also not define *supernatural* so broadly that it means anything that makes us wonder, like sunsets, or babies, or Juliet.

Supernatural means more-than-natural, so we must first define *nature* and *natural*.

What *nature* means most of the time to most people today is the universe, the space-time continuum that contains all the matter that exists, all the stuff that began some twelve to eighteen billion years ago in the "Big Bang".

What most people mean by *God*, then, is supernatural. The pagan gods were not supernatural; they were parts of nature. For instance, Zeus lived on Mount Olympus, or in the sky, or above it; Poseidon lived in the sea. But God is not in one part of nature; he *created* it.

So if you can prove the existence of God, you prove the existence of the supernatural.

You *can* prove the existence of God. There are at least a dozen, perhaps two dozen, good arguments for the existence of God. If you really want to explore them, a short and simple summary can be found in *Handbook of Christian Apologetics* by Kreeft and Tacelli. An even shorter and simpler summary is in my *Fundamentals of the Faith* and an even simpler one in *Yes or No?*

If you can prove the existence of the supernatural, then there is a "place" for angels, a category for them to inhabit.

If there is a God, why not angels? If there is an infinite spirit, why can't there be finite spirits? Why swallow an orange but choke on a kumquat?

I also highly recommend C. S. Lewis' book *Miracles*, which begins by logically refuting naturalism. Summarized, the argument is this: if only nature exists, then when I think and reason and prove things, the only thing that's happening is that atoms are moving in my brain because other atoms pushed them. Human reason is caused only by nature, by the sum total of all the material events, from the Big Bang through evolution to photons of light stimulating my optic nerve to send electrical charges to my brain now. Why should I trust my reasoning, then, if it is caused by nothing but blind, unintelligent material forces? If there is no supernatural Mind, if my material brain is not moved by or in touch with or aware of any superior Spirit or Mind (however many material means and intermediaries he may use), then I have destroyed the credentials of my thinking, including *that* very act of skeptical thinking. Then I can't help how my tongue happens to wag. Then I think a certain thing is true only because atoms and wind and weather and digestion and electricity have necessitated it, not because a wise and good Father God is teaching his children through many material intermediaries, as a teacher teaches students through blackboards and books. If there is no supernatural, then science is like listening to a broadcast of the news when there's no broadcaster, no one on the other end. The television set and the wires are like the universe and our bodies and senses: the *means* of communication. God is like the broadcaster. Would you pay attention if you thought the broadcast just happened and there was *nobody there*? Would you pay attention to your own thinking if you believed it was nothing but the inevitable echoes of the evolutionary belch of the primordial slime?

To change the analogy: suppose you came to believe that your friends were only machines. Would you still think it rational to trust them, to believe them? Suppose they were dead bodies without souls, without minds, but somehow they kept moving and speaking even though they were dead. Would you trust them to tell you the truth? Sometimes corpses move, or sit up, or even belch, because the muscles are relaxing, or because there is something like residual electrical energy left in them, like the "ghost image" on a television screen after you turn the set off. Suppose there was enough energy in a corpse to make the lungs and the tongue move to make the sound "God is". Would that justify your believing that God is? Of course not. *But that's the way things are* if naturalism is true and there is no God teaching us and no image of God, no rational soul, no immaterial spirit in us controlling our brain, commanding our body, receiving and interpreting and understanding the teaching.

Naturalism is a very convenient philosophy for crooks. It means that I am not responsible for anything, for nature made me do it. There is no I, really. I am only complexified primordial slime.

"As a man thinketh in his heart, so is he." Naturalism flattens you out. You're only a clever ape. So why not expect people to act like apes? If you're the king's kid, you'll act kingly. If you're made in the image of King God, you'll act godly. But if you're made in the image of King Kong—well, you can read the papers as well as I can.

9 *Isn't the supernatural unscientific?*

Yes. Science can't prove it.

But it's not *anti*scientific, because science can't *disprove* it either. All the reasonings about all the observations of all the events *within* the system of nature can't disprove something *outside* of nature, something *other* than nature. Nothing a baby bird inside an egg hears or feels or thinks can disprove the world outside the egg. How could it?

There are many things that are "unscientific" but not antiscientific, things science can't prove but can't disprove either—things everyone accepts, like beauty, and love, and morality, and the presence of a self, an "I" in this body, not just atoms. So there's nothing wrong with being "unscientific".

If angels can cause changes in nature—if angels can stop a speeding car in two seconds or appear and disappear in bodies—then the human senses can detect their *effects*, like footprints in the sand. But the *cause* is invisible, since angels are pure spirits. Science cannot observe angels. They don't reflect light.

Miracles are also "unscientific" because their cause is invisible (God or angels, supernatural spirits). But miracles are not *anti*scientific. Science can't disprove them. When you hear someone claim that "science has disproved miracles", please get scientific for a moment. Ask him: "*Which* science? What was the experiment that proved this? Who did it? When? Where?" You will quickly see that the so-called science is not science at all but a religion, a faith. The contest is not between science and faith but between two faiths. It is not scientific argument but spiritual warfare.

10 *Are there any purely logical reasons for believing in angels apart from faith in the data in the Bible and people's stories of meeting angels?*

Yes, but it is only a good probability, not a proof. It is the analogy with animals. We see that the universe is full of all sorts of species. Every possible rung on the cosmic hierarchy is filled. There are no gaps. Below us there are intelligent animals, like apes, then less intelligent animals, like fish, then barely intelligent animals, like slugs and TV producers, then plants, then minerals. The strategy of the Creator seems to be fullness, not emptiness. The universe looks more like a Victorian mansion crammed full of strange overstuffed furniture than a Japanese Zen meditation hall, simple and clean and empty. Well, if there were no angels, there would be a great gap be-

"The Annunciation" (16th cent.)
National Museum, Belgrade

tween us and God, a gap upward on the ladder, even though there is no such fundamental gap downward. Spirits without bodies (angels) are possible just as bodies without spirits (stones) are possible. Why should one be actual but not the other?

Suppose we had just discovered an old manuscript that claimed to be an authentic Socratic dialogue written by Plato. Suppose some scholars believed the claim, and others did not. How would we judge the claim? By analogy to the dialogues we have, the dialogues we all agree are Plato's. Does the Socrates in the questionable dialogue feel like the Socrates in the unquestionable dialogues? We can all intuit, more or less, what "fits" and what doesn't. If the new Socrates were more interested in physics than ethics, or if he dogmatized instead of questioning, or if he were impious and arrogant, we would know that dialogue was not authentic. But if we detected the same spiritual fingerprints on this dialogue as we found in the authentic Platonic dialogues, that would be probable (not certain) evidence for its authenticity. Well, the fingerprints of the Author of plankton and platypuses are on the angels too. They *fit.*

Let's go through this argument again more carefully.

When man reflects on the universe and his place in it and uses common sense, he discovers the principle of hierarchy.

Living things are higher, ontologically better than nonliving things. They have more power, more glory, more beauty. They rightly elicit more wonder. There *is* more in a petal of a rose than in a grain of sand.

Animals are higher than plants. Dogs feel; roses do not. We all act as if we believe in hierarchy; we cut roses off a rosebush, but we do not cut an ear off a dog. Why? Because dogs have feelings, but roses do not. When a dog runs through a rosebush, the rose thorns can hurt the dog, but the dog's claws can't hurt the roses.

As plants are higher than minerals, and animals higher than

plants, man is higher than other animals because he *knows* love, he can love deliberately, he can choose, freely and rationally.

We also observe that within each rung on this cosmic ladder there are subhierarchies. Oak trees are greater, more complex, more developed organisms than seaweed. Apes are more than amoebas. Though there are fundamental differences (mineral, plant, animal, man), they are softened by degrees, so that the ladder looks almost continuous. The highest plant resembles the lowest animal. There are no big gaps.

If there were no animals, there would be a big gap between plants and men; if no plants, a big gap between animals and minerals. And if there were no angels, there would be a big gap between man and God.

It's all very simple and obvious and traditional and commonsensical—or so it seemed until quite recently. It's not a proof, but it's a reasonable argument.

Most arguments most people use for most things most of the time are just like this: only probable, not certain; only "fitting", not proved; only intuitively likely, not mathematically demonstrated. Why should we think this is legitimate for thousands of other things we believe but not for angels? What are we afraid of, anyway?

Of course it's only belief, not proof, but it's reasonable belief. It's much more unreasonable *not* to believe in angels than to believe in them. And that unbelief is also a faith, not a proof.

11 *Why can't there be a logical proof of the existence of angels?*

Because the empirical data we have—angel appearances—can't be proved to be caused by real angels, who are invisible spirits.

The *appearances* of angels are not angels themselves. They are either visions or disguises. (See question 24.)

When we prove the existence of something invisible, we argue from what is visible by the principle of causality, from the visible effect back to the invisible cause. All our knowledge begins with the visible, with sense experience. To know beyond our sense experience we must argue by this principle of causality, and we must show that *only* such and such an invisible cause could account for the observed visible effects.

We can do this with God but not with angels. For the effects that angels produce (rescues, for example) cannot be proved to have been caused by angels and only angels, as the effects of God—the universe—can be proved to have been caused by God and only God. Nothing but a First Uncaused Cause could cause the whole chain of second caused causes that is the universe. But other things *could* have caused the visible works that angels perform.

12 *Are angels* necessary?

No. That's why pure reason can't prove their existence, as it can prove necessary truths like "being exists" or "effects need causes" or "2 + 3 = 5" or "good should be done and evil should not". Angels are like animals: God did not have to create them.

Question 9 explains *why* God created angels, but that's not the same thing as proving he did it, and it's certainly not proving that he had to. God created freely. No beings are necessary except God. Nothing else *has* to be; everything else is "contingent". Everything that was not created (like a green tiger) is a might-have-been, and everything that was created (like an orange tiger) is a might-not-have-been. It is a sheer gift, a sheer grace. That is true of each angel and each animal, and it is true of you. Only free generosity, altruism, and love could have motivated God to create a universe that he did not need (if he's absolutely and unqualifiedly perfect, he doesn't need anything outside himself). He acted like a parent having a big family.

Some philosophers have tried to prove the necessity of angels by arguing as follows:

> A perfect God would necessarily create the best of all possible worlds.
> A world with angels is more perfect than a world without them.
> Therefore God created angels.

The problem with that argument is first of all the word *necessarily.* As we just saw, God created freely, not necessarily. Second, there is no such thing as the "best of all possible worlds", just as there is no such thing as the "highest finite number". You can always add one more perfection to any finite perfection, just as you can always add one more integer to any finite number.

13 *Why do people believe in angels?*

Here are seven possible reasons, ranging from the worst to the best:

1. They want to. It feels good. It's fun.
2. They think they need to—like believing in cops when you walk through a dark urban alley.
3. Intuition.
4. Philosophical reasoning—for example, the argument in question 10.
5. They knew someone who met one and believe his word.
6. They met one themselves.

7. They believe God's word. Jesus, the Bible, and the Church all assure us angels are real. Why not believe them? Are we wiser than they? What do we know, anyway?

14 *Why do many people think it's stupid to believe in angels?*

One reason is a mistake about themselves: the failure to distinguish between (1) sense perception or imagination (which is a kind of inner sensing) and (2) reason, or intelligence, or understanding. We don't *see* pure spirits, and we can't *imagine* them. That doesn't mean we can't *know* or *understand* them. We can see and imagine the difference between a five-sided figure (a pentagon) and a six-sided figure (a hexagon), and we can also intellectually understand that difference. We cannot, however, sense or imagine the difference between a 105-sided figure and a 106-sided figure. Both *look* to us simply like circles. But we can *understand* the difference and even measure it exactly. So we can understand some things we can't see. We can't see qualities like good and evil either. What color or shape or size is evil? Yet we can understand them. We can imagine our brains, but not our minds, our personalities. But we can know them.

Many who deny angels deny or are unaware of the spiritual half of themselves. Angels are a touchstone of "know thyself". So are animals.

15 *Why not believe in God without angels? Who needs angels?*

We don't believe in angels just because we need them or because we need faith in them. To believe in something only be-

"St. Peter Rescued by an Angel" (detail)
RAPHAEL
St. Peter inside the Walls, Vatican City

cause you need it or because you need faith is to be confused or dishonest. The only clear and honest reason for believing anything is that it is true, it is there. That's the reason to believe in angels: the same reason to believe in platypuses. We don't need them either, but they're there.

If you have no trouble believing in God and your own soul, what's the problem with angels? God is infinite bodiless spirit, your soul is finite embodied spirit, and angels are finite bodiless spirits.

If the reason you believe in God is because you are a Jew, a Christian, or a Muslim, then you must believe in angels, since all three religions teach the reality of angels. If you believe the Bible is God's word to man, not man's word about God, then you believe in angels, for the Bible says they are real. If you believe in Jesus, even as a mere human prophet, then you believe in angels, for Jesus assures you they are real (Mt 13:39, 41, 49; 16:27; 18:10; 22:30; 24:31, 36; 25:31, 41; 26:53; Mk 8:38; 12:25; 13:27, 32; Lk 4:10; 9:26; 12:8, 9; 15:10; 16:22; 20:36; Jn 1:51).

16 *What about the opposite: believing not in God without angels but in angels without God?*

If many great superhuman spirits exist, why shouldn't the Great Spirit exist? Why not their Creator?

There are no good *reasons* for believing in angels without God, but there are powerful *motives*. They essentially come down to comfort. It's just the right faith for yuppies.

Today, most people who don't believe in God are not hard-headed scientists who demand rational proof of everything, but softhearted, compassionate people who are afraid God is too tough, too demanding, too "judgmental", too moralistic. The primary reason for refusing to believe in God—the God of Judaism, Christianity, and Islam—is *moral* today.

Some of these people today who don't believe in God do believe in angels.

For angels do not give us a Ten Commandments. When we open our inner door and enter the holy room of an honest conscience, we don't meet angels there.

God is an interferer, like the prophets, like parents. Angels can be distant heroes, like sports superstars.

Furthermore, according to many of the recent angel books, angels are *comfortable*. They are not fearsome. They are not even "judgmental". In other words, they are very different from the angels described in the Bible. Every time one appears *there*, it has to say "fear not". There is something fearsome about those angels. (See question 34.)

17 *Can you be a Christian without believing in angels?*

Angels are not at the very center of Christianity; Christ is. To be a Christian is essentially to believe in Jesus Christ as the Son of God and the Savior.

But Jesus clearly taught the existence of angels. (See question 15.) So if angels don't exist, Jesus was in error; if Jesus was in error, he was not divine and infallible; and if he was not divine and infallible, Christianity is essentially false. So to be a Christian includes believing in angels.

Or perhaps the question means: Can you be saved, can you go to heaven, without believing in angels? Yes. You don't get to heaven by believing in angels. You get to heaven by believing in Jesus, by repenting of sin and accepting God's forgiveness.

Or perhaps the question means: Can you be a good person without believing in angels? Of course. But "Christian" does not mean "good person". Some Christians are not very good people, and some very good people are not professing Christians.

All orthodox Christians believe the teachings of the Bible, and angels are clearly taught throughout the Bible. Catholics also believe all the public, official, creedal, binding teachings of the Church. These are *de fide*, of faith—not *my* faith but *the* Faith, the public, universal Catholic Faith. This includes angels. Angels are *de fide*. The Fourth Lateran Council explicitly declared that. So to be a believing Catholic is to believe (among other things) in angels. If angels are myths, the Church has been teaching error and she is not what she claims to be. In that case, she may be in error on other issues, on any issue.

As to *what* Catholics must believe about angels and about anything else, the new *Catechism of the Catholic Church* is the clearest and most recent definitive work to answer that question. Next to the Bible, it should be every Catholic's primary reference book today.

PART THREE

QUESTIONS ABOUT THE NATURE OF ANGELS

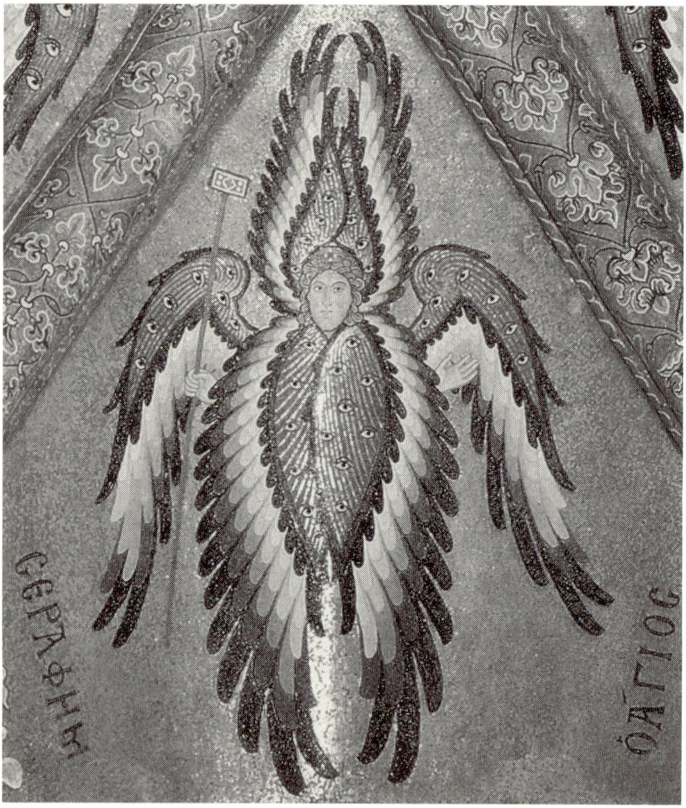

Seraphim with eyes on wings
"Celestial Hierarchy" (detail)
Duomo Cefalu, Italy

18 *Of what are angels made?*

Everything in the material universe is made of something: subatomic particles, at least. But not angels. They are not *in* this universe of matter, space, and time, not made of matter. They have no parts; that's why they can never fall apart and die or be destroyed, as we can. They are pure spirits, not any kind of matter or physical energy at all—not light or ectoplasm or auras or anything visible or tangible.

Angels don't belong in this universe. (They're *visitors*.) But you don't totally belong here either. You also have a part of you beyond matter and space and time. That doesn't make you an angel. But your spirit side—your soul, mind, intellect, will, emotions—is *like* an angel. We all have inside us the need to find that mountain in *Close Encounters*. We're just not 100 percent at home here.

19 *How can angels be anything at all if they have no bodies? We can't imagine a spirit without a body.*

We can conceive of all sorts of things we can't imagine, such as time, and relationships, and numbers. You can imagine a just person, but you can't imagine Justice. You can imagine two apples, but you can't imagine twoness. You can imagine a body, but not a spirit, or mind, or soul. You can't imagine your self, only your body.

Many people disbelieve in angels because they disbelieve in spirit. They believe only matter exists. The technical name for this philosophy is materialism. Materialism, the denial of spirit or soul, is a faith. It is not scientific, for there can be no scientific proof against something that cannot appear as data for any scientific instrument.

Materialism is not commonsensical, for fewer than one percent of all men in history have believed it.

Materialism is not based on experience, for we experience our minds as well as our bodies.

Humans are the lowest (least intelligent) of spirits and the highest (most intelligent) of animals. We are rational animals, incarnate minds, the smartest of animals and the stupidest of spirits:

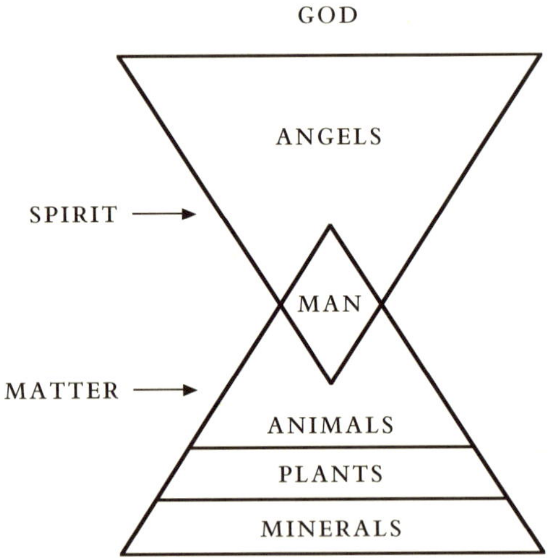

20 *Can you prove spirit exists? Can you prove materialism is untrue?*

1. Nonmaterialists don't demand of materialists that they prove matter is real. Why does the materialist demand that we prove that spirit is real?

2. We appeal to common experience. Most people experience both their bodies *and* their souls, or spirits, or minds.

3. Materialism is insulting. If it is true, we are only sophisticated animals or machines.

4. If you are a machine, then you can't change or control what you do any more than the ecosystem of the earth can help evaporating water. All acts of thinking and choosing are nothing but movements of atoms, or material energy, like gravity or electricity. How then can some of these atom movements be *true* and others *false*? You don't say that the evaporation that happens on the surface of one lake is *true* and the evaporation that happens on the surface of another lake is *false*. They simply both happen. So if acts of thinking are just material events that happen, like evaporation, it makes no sense to call some true and others false. In that case, it makes no sense to call the thought of materialism true and of non-materialism false. The theory contradicts itself; it undercuts itself. If it is true, nothing is true, including it. Matter is not *true*; matter is neither true nor false; matter just is. If nothing but matter exists, then nothing is true, including the thought of materialism.

5. You can't prove a lot of things that it would be lunacy to deny—for instance, that human reason is trustworthy, that it is not being hypnotized by a demon at every moment. Of course that thought is ridiculous, but can you prove it isn't true? No, because you'd have to use your reason to prove it, and that means trusting the validity of reason, and that is assuming the very thing you're supposed to be proving, "begging the question". If a thousand prisoners are all on trial, no one of them has the right to be the judge and declare all one thousand innocent. If all acts of reasoning are on trial and need to be justified, no one of them has the right to do that justifying. So you can't prove the validity of reasoning. So not everything has to be proved, for not everything *can* be proved. So the demand to prove the existence of spirit, and the refusal to believe it just because it isn't proved, is an unfair demand.

6. If there is no spirit, there is no God. But God can be proved. (See question 8.) Therefore, there is spirit.

7. OBEs (out-of-body experiences) are real, and they disprove materialism. Materialism says that the mind is only the brain. (That's like saying that the computer user is just a computer, or a speaker is just a microphone, or a swordsman is just a sword.) But you *can* think without a brain! Millions have done it. When they were out of their bodies, their brain was "dead" and not acting. Yet they were doing a lot of thinking and knowing and even perceiving things going on in the other rooms of the hospital, for example, or the location of hidden or lost objects. If you doubt this evidence, just visit the University of Connecticut in Storrs, Connecticut. You will be impressed by the quality and quantity of the evidence for OBEs that has been scientifically collected there.

21 *What is this "spirit" of which angels are made?*

Spirit means essentially two things:

1. The power of thinking—conscious, deliberate, rational understanding. Not sense perception; that's the work of a bodily organ, like the eye.
2. The power of willing and choosing and deliberately loving. Not sensory appetite; that's the work of a bodily function, like hunger.

God and angels are pure spirits. Humans and intelligent extraterrestrials (if there are any) are spirit-body compounds.

22 *Are angels human souls without bodies? Are they the same as ghosts?*

No, angels aren't humans without bodies any more than fish are birds without wings. They're a different *kind*, a different *species* of mind, or intelligence, just as man is a different species of animal than fish.

Human souls are meant for bodies. Angels are not.

Human souls and angels (pure spirits) are easily confused with each other because both are immaterial. Neither one has size or color. Neither one has parts. (Therefore neither one can ever die, both are immortal.) And neither one has weight. (There have been attempts to weigh the soul by registering the weight loss from a body at the moment of death by putting the deathbed on a very delicate scale. No verifiable result has ever been produced.)

The word *soul* has been used in four different ways; three correct and one incorrect:

1. The source of life in plant, animal, or man; what makes the difference between life and death in any organism; the "life-force" or life-energy.
2. The source of desire, which plants don't have but animals and men do—like your cat's desire to sleep on your head.
3. The human, rational soul, with its powers of thinking, willing, and feeling.
4. Any spirit, including angels. (This is an improper use of the word *soul*.)

Ghosts are the spirits, or souls, of *human beings* whose bodies have died. They may hover around the earth "haunting" material places, usually houses. There seem to be four possible reasons for this:

1. They don't yet realize they are dead.
2. They were so attached to their material places or possessions that they can't detach themselves from them and leave.
3. They are working out some purification, penance, or purgatory, some remedial education or "reform school".
4. They are consoling their loved ones who have been bereaved.

Angels, in contrast, did not have human bodies in the first place and never will. Ghosts once had human bodies and will receive new resurrection bodies in heaven if they go there.

23 *If angels have no bodies, how can we ever see them?*

Angels sometimes "assume" bodies, as we would put on a costume or hire a tuxedo or a limo.

At other times angels influence our imagination from within, like hypnosis or mental telepathy. Then it *looks* as if there is a body there, but there isn't. In this case, a camera would not record anything. It would in the first case, if they "assumed" bodies.

If you are ever visited by an angel and wonder whether it is objective or subjective, without or within, here is how to tell. Angels respect hospitality, so offer the angel some food. (It doesn't have to be angel food cake, but Miss Manners would think it very rude to offer them devil's food cake.) Count the cakes, or candies, or cookies, and after the angel has left count again. If one more is missing than the ones you ate, then the angel assumed a body.

(This advice is not my invention; it comes from the very practical Jewish tradition.)

The bodies angels assume are not literal, living human bodies. They did not come out of a mother's womb. They don't *have* to eat or breathe. They did not grow; they were manufactured by spirits. They are masks.

Some philosophers believe that angels never assume bodies, that all angelic appearances to men, including those recorded in the Bible, are only inner visions that take place within the imagination. Saint Thomas Aquinas argues against this opinion in this way: "What is seen only in someone's imagination is a purely private experience; it is not a thing that anyone else can see at the same time. But the Scriptures speak of angels appearing visibly to everyone who happened to be present at a given place: those seen by Abraham, for example, were also seen by his servant, and those seen by Lot were also seen by the people of Sodom" (ST I, 51, 2).

24 *What have angels done in past history?*

Angels were created before the dawn of time.

They sang at the creation of the world.

Some rebelled against God, became demons, or devils (evil spirits), and set up hell's lowerarchy against heaven's hierarchy.

One of them was the snake in the grass that tempted us to give up paradise.

Angels were instrumental at every major stage of God's plan to get us back on the road to paradise. They surrounded the life of Abraham, the first of God's "chosen people". They announced to Sarah, his hundred-year-old, laughing wife, that she would have a miracle baby. They stopped him from making a human sacrifice of Isaac. They saved Abraham and his nephew Lot from the foretaste of hell that destroyed Sodom and Gomorrah. They came to Jacob in the desert on a ladder, back and forth like eighteen-wheelers on that busy highway to heaven. One picked up the prophet Habbakuk by the hair and whisked him seven hundred miles away.

Angels came to old women and old men, to the blind and the poor, to shepherds and fleeing criminals, but not to kings or politicians. One came to a teenaged Jewish girl as an ambassador of her Creator and meekly asked her permission in his name to use her womb as his door into our world. And because she said Yes to his angel, we have Christmas, and Easter, and the hope of heaven.

And when the Creator became a shivering, hairless, wet little baby, surrounded by scruffy sheep and drooling cows, they exploded over the night sky like a million close-encountered mother ships. And when, 33 years later, he had to muster up the courage in the garden of Gethsemane to jump into the corss-shaped pit of hell, they were there to comfort him.

And when he burst the doors of the dead wide open, they were there at the stone door to announce it to the women (who in turn, playing angel, as they always have, relayed it to the slower men). And when he leaped back home into the sky, they reminded his friends, who stood gaping up at the gap in the sky, that he would return and that they had better get busy spending the rest of history getting his landing field ready.

And when he comes again, they will be there, blowing the sky in half with their trumpets and taking us home when Daddy calls to put away our toys. As they sang time's beginning, they will sing its end when the firmament is folded back like a book turned to its last page: "The end."

25 *Do we become angels after we die?*

No. We don't change species. God didn't make a mistake when he made us human. He doesn't rip up his design but perfects it.

We don't become angels any more than we become apes. We don't evolve into angels either, even if we may have evolved from apes, because evolution is only a theory about the origin of *biological* species. There can be no genetics and no "natural selection", no "survival of the fittest", for pure spirits.

Don't take your theology from Hollywood; that's like using the Bible to learn how to run a movie studio.

26 *Didn't Jesus say in the Bible (Matthew 22) that we would be "like the angels in heaven"?*

Jesus said not that we would *be* angels or *become* angels but that we would be *like* angels. Now in what way will we be like angels? You must look at the context. The Sadducees, who asked Jesus the question, didn't believe in heaven, life after death, angels, miracles, or the supernatural. The question they asked Jesus was about *marriage* in heaven. They thought they were being funny and mocking the idea of heaven by asking Jesus whose wife a woman would be in heaven if she had seven husbands on earth. Jesus' reply was simply that no one gets married in heaven. *That's* the way we will be like angels. They were *not* asking Jesus about *bodies* in heaven. If they had asked that, he would never have said that we would be bodiless, like the angels, for he himself ascended to heaven *with his resurrected body.*

The resurrection of the body is a fundamental Christian dogma. It is one of the twelve articles of the oldest and most basic creed, the Apostles' Creed. Orthodox Judaism has also always believed it. So do Muslims.

27 *If angels come from heaven, what is "heaven"?*

"Heaven" can mean at least five different (but related) things:

1. A human state of mind, intense joy. ("Oh, I'm in heaven!") This "heaven" can mean anything you want—chocolates, for instance. If heaven is only a state of mind, it isn't any more objectively real than Santa Claus. Angels don't come from this heaven, from your mind, like Santa Claus. They aren't myths or metaphors. They are real.
2. The sky, the firmament, what you see outdoors when you

look up. No one thinks angels are birds, so this is not the "heaven" angels come from.

3. Outer space. But angels are not material creatures from other planets in outer space. They don't come in flying saucers.
4. The "place" beyond outer space where God lives, the place you hope to go to after you die, the alternative to hell. This is the place orthodox Christians, Jews, and Muslims believe God, angels, and saints (saved souls) inhabit. This is a real *place*, but not a material *space* somewhere in the universe. You can't get to heaven in a rocket ship.
5. The very inner life of God, God's mind. This "heaven" is proper to God alone, but Christians believe God—incredibly—has chosen to share it with men through Christ the God-Man, who has both human life and divine life. Thus, if they accept this gift of being adopted into God's family and becoming Christ's brothers, men are exalted even above angels! Angels have only angel life, which is superhuman but subdivine. But the blessed, the saved, those humans who go to heaven, have human *and divine* life, like Christ. They become little Christs—*very* little Christs, yet very little *Christs.*

28 *Do angels have different personalities?*

Yes! More so than men, in fact. Angels are more individually different than we are, for each angel is a distinct *species*, as different from another angel as cats from dogs.

The reason for this is that it is *matter* that multiplies a species into many individuals, as paper multiplies a letter into many copies in a photocopier. The essential *form* is the same. We are all essentially human. What makes us many is our matter. Now, since angels have no matter, there can be only one angel for each species or form.

All Asians, or all Africans, may look alike to someone who is unfamiliar with Asians, or Africans. We are *unfamiliar* with angels. They are so different from us that they all seem alike.

But they aren't. There are far more possibilities for spiritual differences in personalities than for material differences in bodies. Spirits have more possibilities for nearly everything than do bodies—for example, more pleasures and pains, and more subtle and profound pleasures and pains, than bodies. The same is true of personalities.

Gabriel and Michael and Raphael (the three angels named in the Bible) are more like Dog and Cat and Bird than like Lassie and Fido and Spot.

Therefore, angels are arranged in a vertical hierarchy. There is no equality among angels, no angel twins.

Imagine a military ranking: four-star general, three-star general, and so on down to buck private. Now expand the number of ranks to billions. (For there are at least as many angels as men—one guardian angel for every human being who has ever lived.) Now reduce the population of each rank to just one. (For each angel is a separate rank or species.) Now you have the angel army.

All humans are essentially equal, unequal only in nonessentials like age, wealth, or color. Many deny this in practice by treating severely handicapped people, terminally ill people, old and "useless" people, and very small, unseen, undeveloped people—the unborn—as nonhuman *things* to kill rather than persons to love and respect and accept. The root reason for this is the denial of the human essence, the human equality, the human family—judging people's worth only by how efficiently or intelligently or quickly they *function*. This is confusing the essence with the nonessential.

29 *According to traditional angelology, angels are supposed to form a* hierarchy. *Why? Isn't this just a projection of medieval monarchical politics?*

1. The alternative notion that angels are equal could as well be just a projection of modern egalitarian politics.

2. One reason to believe that angels are ranked in a hierarchy is tradition and authority. These are two emotionally negative words today, especially in individualistic cultures like America ("we don't do kings here"). And yet nearly everything we know, we have learned from some tradition and some authority.

3. And then there is the *beauty* of the idea. "The Nine Choirs of Angels" (question 45) is an artistic masterpiece of cosmic architecture. It has inspired poets like Dante and Milton, philosophers like Dionysius the Areopagite and Aquinas, artists like Raphael and Michelangelo, and through them millions of souls. Of course, that does not prove it is true, but it shows that it is not to be cavalierly dismissed.

4. There is a philosophical reason (found in Thomas Aquinas) why angels must form a "vertical" hierarchy rather than a "horizontal" equality. Two men or two dogs are essentially equal because their identical essence (or nature, or species, or form, or "whatness") is realized in two different bits of matter. But angels have no matter, no bodies. They are pure spirits, pure minds, pure forms. Therefore no two of them can be identical and equal, any more than two forms or species can—for example, dog and cat, or tree and flower. Two dogs are equal in essence, but dog and cat are not. They are two different essences.

So there are no angel twins. Each angel is a species, or the only member of its species. And if no two angels are equal, they must be *unequal*, one superior and the other inferior *by their different essences*. Human beings are unequal only in nonessential ("accidental") qualities. Each angel is inferior or superior to every other angel. From the fact that angels are pure spirits it logically follows that they are unequal.

30 *Hierarchy and inequality among angels sound unjust and unfair. Is God an elitist?*

1. God's justice is not equality. Neither is nature's.

God the Creator is not equal to any of his creatures, but he is supreme.

Among his creatures, spiritual creatures (angels and men) are superior to merely biological creatures.

Among spiritual creatures, angels are more intelligent than men.

Even within our own species, men are not all equal in intelligence, in quickness, in wisdom, in memory, or in many other things.

And, of course, humans are superior to animals. If you doubt this, you'd better stop eating fish or start eating humans.

Higher (more intelligent) animals are superior to lower (less intelligent) animals. That's why we prefer dogs to worms as pets. Even biologists rank species in a hierarchical order. The more complex they are, the more conscious they are and the more sophisticated their functions.

2. The hierarchy of angels over men parallels the hierarchy of men over animals, and the hierarchy within angels parallels the hierarchy within animals. If the arrangement of animals tells us something about the Creator's style and principles and preferences, it's reasonable to expect to find his style and principles and preferences manifested in angels too.

3. Justice does not mean equality, even among men. It means treating unequals unequally—giving an A to a student who answered 95 out of 100 questions correctly and an F to a student who answered only 45.

Many traditional societies, like those of classical Greece and Confucian China, saw justice as essentially an *inequality*, a harmony among *different* things: organs in the body, members in a family, heavenly bodies in the cosmos, musical notes in a song, classes in the state, faculties in the soul. The President is not necessarily a superior *person* to his military chief of staff, but his *office* is. Justice demands the chief of staff obey his "superior", even if the latter has shortcomings.

4. Resentment against some kind of superiority is one of the seven deadly sins. It is called envy, and it is the only sin that never gave anyone any kind of pleasure at all.

In the *Divine Comedy*, Dante discovers that there are many unequal levels even in heaven. He asks Piccarda, who is on heaven's lowest level, whether she is not discontented with her lowly place and whether she longs to move up closer to God, to see more of God and receive more joy. Her answer is that no one in heaven is dissatisfied with his place or envious of anyone else: "From seat to seat throughout this realm, to all the realm is pleasing. [That is, each citizen is pleased with the kingdom as a whole; the whole is present to each individual.] For in his will our hearts have found their peace."

T. S. Eliot called this the profoundest line in all human literature.

31 *What's the most fascinating description of angels in literature? What do you most recommend that I read?*

The contest is not even close, in my book. The first prize goes to C. S. Lewis' space trilogy—*Out of the Silent Planet, Perelandra*, and *That Hideous Strength*—which depicts angels as *other*, as formidable, as awesome. Lewis invents new symbols for them: pillars of light, of no earthly color, at an angle that makes straight lines on earth seem crooked. Five of them parallel classical gods: Wordsmith (Mercury), Lover (Venus), Warrior (Mars), Joviality (Jupiter), and Eternal Oldness (Saturn).

The second prize goes to Tolkien's *Silmarillion*, where angels sing the universe into being.

32 *Are angels involved in politics?*

Yes! There are guardian angels not only for each individual, according to Scripture (Mt 18:10), but also for communities: cities and states. Probably every real (as distinct from artificial) community has its guardian angel. These are called "principalities". (See Daniel 10.) Principalities oversee great changes in kingdoms. Behind the wars on earth there may be wars in heaven (see Dan 10, Rev 12:7).

Upon reflection it seems not such a strange idea after all. Doesn't there often seem to be an unknown, unpredictable, invisible factor in history, especially in times of physical or spiritual conflict, "culture wars" or spiritual warfare (*jihad*)? If angels live up to their name as "messengers" and actually run errands for God here in this world, they must influence lives collectively as well as individually. They make a difference; they are a cause of historical events. Not the only cause, of course, but a real cause nevertheless.

In times like these it would seem fitting and prudent to pray for the protection of the guardian angel of America. He has been losing a lot of battles lately.

In the nine "choirs" of angels (question 45), the higher angels are apolitical—they remain in heaven and contemplate God—but the lower angels, especially the guardian angels, have tasks in human life and history.

But though there is an angel for each real, concrete community, there are no angels for political parties.

33 *Are angels comforting?*

In the end, yes, but not always in the beginning.

All the current angel books seem to assume that angels are comforting. Yet almost every time a real angel appears in the Bible, he has to say "Fear not!" And angels do not use superfluous words. Like Jesus and unlike popular spiritualists and occultists, they are laconic.

Religious *fear*, or awe, is an essential ingredient of all true religion, yet it has been systematically exiled from modern, "psychologically correct" religion. What irony!—the thing the Bible calls the "beginning of wisdom" is the experience modern religious educators and liturgists deliberately remove or try to remove from our souls: fear and trembling, adoration and worship, the bent knee and the prone heart. The modern God is "something I can feel comfortable with". The God of the Bible, in contrast, is "a consuming fire". (See Psalm 103[104]:4 and Hebrews 12:29).

Angels are closer to God, and something of his fiery fearsomeness rubs off on them. Rabbi Abraham Heschel, when told by a student that it must be gratifying to spend his life amid "the comforts of religion", replied, "God is not an uncle. God is not nice. God is an earthquake." The same applies to God's angels.

Of course God and his angels are *good*. But "good" does not mean "comfortable". "Aslan is not a tame lion." When you meet him, you "go all trembly".

And of course "fear" does not mean "craven fear" or "fear of an evil tyrant". It means awe. But this is much more than "respect", which is how the biblical term *fear* is usually interpreted today. No. You don't just "respect" God. You "respect" the value of money, or the power of an internal combustion engine, or the conventions of politeness, or a handicap. You smile politely and take account of it. Only a fool does that to God. Refusal to fall flat on your face proves that the God you have met is simply not the real God.

However, angels don't *always* inspire fear. Sometimes they disguise themselves as humans (see question 23), presumably for that very reason, to overcome the fear that people would otherwise naturally have when they meet a real angel without a human disguise.

Angels (as distinct from devils—fallen angels) always do us good. They warn, rescue, guide, and enlighten. So the end result is indeed comforting. But not at first. True religion never begins in comfort. It begins in repentance and humility and fear.

34 *What do angels do all day? Don't they get bored?*

Angels have no "days", no chronological time. That's relative to matter, and they have no matter.

Therefore angels don't get bored. To be bored, you have to be in time. Boredom comes from waiting around doing nothing. Angels never wait.

Well, what do they do for all eternity, then?

Have insights. Insights just keep popping into their minds, a neverending stream. They are like super scientists, artists, poets, and philosophers.

Angels are intuitive intelligences. They "just know" and contemplate what they know: God, themselves, each other, and us: *persons.*

Since persons are unending subjects, not finite objects that come to an end, angels never get bored with them. Neither do we. The only thing that never gets boring is persons, for persons are inexhaustible.

Angels also love, because love follows knowledge. (This is will-love, not feeling-love. See question 56.) Angels know and therefore love God, themselves, each other, and us.

"Angels in Adoration" (detail)
GOZZOLI BENOZZO (d. 1497)
Palazzo Medici Riccardi

We will do the same eight things forever in heaven without being bored—know and love God, angels, each other, and ourselves—forever finding and appreciating layer after layer of the cosmic onion in a love-in that is "the never-ending story".

35 *How do angels "just have insights"?*

The same thing happens to us on a much smaller scale. Sometimes, insights just "pop into our mind". This does not seem weird to us. That's what minds are *for.*

In fact, we must seem weirder to angels than they seem to us, because we have a little of what they have (intelligence), but they have none of what we have (bodies and senses). From the human point of view, angels are fantastic; but suppose you reverse your point of view and take angelic intelligence as the norm. From that point of view, consider how weird we must seem—like philosophical dust or saintly oysters. Animal bodies that think!

36 *How do angels communicate with each other?*

We can deduce the answer to this question from the answer to two others: (1) What are angels made of? and (2) What makes angels individual?

(1) Angels are made of pure spirit (mind and will) without matter, without bodies. Therefore they must communicate by mental telepathy.

This is not fantastic. It appears even in our experience. Haven't you ever concentrated your attention on someone in front of you on a bus or in a line and seen that person instantly turn around to look?

Angels have no bodies, therefore no senses, no sense experience, and no learning from sense experience. If they know visible objects, it is through not sensation but purely mental awareness—something that would be miraculous if it occurred with us. But to angels it is natural, not miraculous or supernatural.

Angels learn from the top down, so to speak: from abstract universal ideas to concrete specific things. We learn mostly from the bottom up, from sense experience of concrete things, through abstracting general principles from them.

Angels communicate immediately, mind to mind, without any medium like air or ears or even words—direct mental telepathy. We communicate mediately, in two ways: through sensible things, such as pictures or audible sounds, and through step-by-step reasoning. We move from "all men are mortal" and "I am a man" to "therefore I am mortal". Angels just see it all at once; they see all the individual applications of the general principle *in* the general principle instead of taking time to reason it out.

(2) Since angels are not equal, as we are (see question 29), therefore they communicate not "horizontally", like equal brothers, but "vertically", like unequal commanders and commanded. They send truth down the hierarchy, and the lower angels receive it from the higher ones, like a human army.

Probably, angels are stocked with innate knowledge from the moment of their creation, like a preprogrammed computer—not knowledge of particular sensible things, like the size of this book, but knowledge of universal principles, such as morality, geometry, and metaphysics.

Like computers, not all angels are equally smart. There are relatively stupid angels—though the stupidest angel is as much smarter than the smartest human as Forrest Gump is smarter than King Kong.

The smarter angels "see" more applications or conclusions

of their universal principles; the less smart ones see fewer. Similarly, not all humans are equally smart. Some of us just understand more than others do.

37 *How do angels communicate with God?*

Angels communicate with God by "reading his mind". They see in God, as in a mirror, whatever they see. Whatever God lets them see, they see. They "just see it". God tells them all they need to know about what's going on in our world; they don't learn it through sense experience. Where we see God reflected in the world, as an artist is reflected in his art, angels see the world reflected in God's mind, somewhat as a listener would see the events of a story told to him by its author.

38 *How do angels communicate with us?*

Usually angels do not communicate directly with us but work behind the scenes, so to speak.

Just as a lot of a play goes on behind the scenes, "in the wings", so in your life a lot of the stuff that's going on, a lot of the action, the spiritual warfare, is going on backstage, invisibly, "in the wings" of good and evil spirits. No one knows just how much, but it seems a safe bet that it's a lot more than we dream of.

When angels do communicate with us, it's usually by suggesting things to our imagination—what we often call "inspiration". However, although they may *suggest* certain thoughts or feelings or actions to us, neither good nor evil spirits can force our mind or will, which are free. (See questions 64 and 65.)

Even God does not force his way in. He's a gentleman. Thus our free will is both the most precious and the most dangerous gift of God.

Angels can also communicate directly to our senses by assuming bodily form, though this is rare, like miracles. (See question 23.)

39 Where *are angels? Where do they live?*

Not in space. Space contains bodies, not spirits.

Yet angels are sometimes seen in definite places and sometimes make things happen in definite places. This is not because angels are present there as matter is but because they are spiritually present. What does that mean? Spirit is mind and will, so spiritual presence is attention and willing. An angel can focus his mind and will on one place in space, somewhat as a telescope can focus the light of the stars, many light-years away, on an eyepiece or a photographic plate. Angels can operate on earth without leaving heaven, somewhat as the sun shines on the earth without losing its place at the center of the solar system ninety-three million miles away from earth.

Space and matter cannot surround or contain spirit. It's vice versa. In us, the soul contains the body rather than the body containing the soul. If our bodies contained our souls, then our souls would have to have physical size. Bodies contain organs such as brains, but not souls. A parallel case: a school contains classrooms; the classrooms do not contain the school. What gives these rooms their form (essence, meaning) is that they are *school* rooms. The general principle is that the essence or formula or form contains matter; matter does not contain form. So angels (spirits) contain the material space in which they work, rather than vice versa.

Another parallel that may illuminate this is a play. The material setting of the play—the stage sets, furniture, costumes, and so on—does not contain the play, but rather the play contains the physical setting as one of its four ingredients (plot, character, setting, theme). So angels "contain" (surround) the space in which they operate, which is something like the setting of the play they perform.

So angels can be present, but not as we are. They can come and go instantly. We can send our thought instantly to any place, even another galaxy, but we cannot be present there in our personal being. Angels can. Nothing physical can move faster than light, but angels can move faster than light, because they are not physical but spiritual.

Thus the James Taylor song "You Just Call Out My Name" can be truly sung only by a guardian angel: "You know, wherever I am, I'll come running to see you . . . ." Only an angel can really say—and mean—"All you got to do is call and I'll be there . . . You've got a friend."

I don't know whether Taylor consciously meant the song to be about a guardian angel or not. If not, maybe his guardian angel pulled off a bit of tricky unconscious inspiration.

Guardian angels come instantly, but they never wholly leave. (See question 82.)

40 *How do angels move?*

Like electrons, in a surprising way.

Scientists tell us that an electron can move from one orbit around its nucleus in the atom onto another orbit *without ever passing through the space between and without taking up any time at all*, instantaneously.

Angels too move in quantum leaps, like a quantum radio

dial. It's called "quantum" because it's like whole numbers: there's no whole number between 2 and 3, as there's no degree of volume between the second and third click on your quantum radio dial. It's not a *continuum* of gradual increase. Angels, having no bodies, are not in the "space-time continuum" that is the material universe, so they don't glide gradually (or continuously) *through* space and time. They pop! like strobe lights.

This sounds incredible, but if even matter can do this at an elementary level (electrons), where it seems to be more like pure energy than hard matter, then why couldn't angels do it, who exist on the highest level, that of pure spirit?

The idea that angels move instantaneously from one place to another without passing through any space or time in between is an idea as old as Saint Thomas Aquinas in the thirteenth century. Mortimer Adler says that when he explained Saint Thomas' theory of how angels move to Niels Bohr, the great twentieth-century quantum physicist, Bohr was amazed and said, "That's exactly the point of modern quantum theory. So a thirteenth-century theologian discovered one of the basic principles of modern nuclear physics seven hundred years ago!" Aquinas deduced from philosophical principles a kind of movement that modern science induced from observation and experiment.

41 *How many angels can dance on the head of a pin?*

Nearly everyone who asks this famous question uses it as a joke against medieval philosophers, who supposedly wasted their time and energy debating such silly questions. Well, if you think that, then you are the pinhead. In the first place, no medieval philosopher ever debated this question. It was a cavil invented by the Protestant Reformers against medieval scholastic philosophers. In the second place, it's a very good question. For it's about us, about our very essence, about the relation between body and soul, matter and spirit. It asks whether place confines spirit.

Since place does not confine spirit, any number of angels can dance (mentally, not physically) on the head of a pin at the same time. But if a pinhead is one undivided place, then only one angel can dance there at once—not because there isn't enough room for more but because, since spirit contains space, one finite spirit will contain one place at one time. An angel occupies a place by surrounding it with his power. The place does not surround the angel, as it surrounds a body; the angel surrounds it. So if a pinhead is one place, only one angel can dance there, alone.

At least, that's the answer given by Thomistic philosophers wiser than I am. I must confess I have some doubts about this answer. Two people can concentrate on the same place at the same time, so why can't two angels? Two people can exercise their mental power on the same place at the same time—for example, both loving the same woman, or both hating the same lawyer—so why can't two angels? When they do spiritual battle, they must cooperate; why not when they "dance"?

42 *What do angels really look like?*

1. Since they are bodiless spirits, the answer is: in themselves, by themselves, they look like nothing. They are invisible.

2. However, they can make themselves look like anything they want, either by manipulating our imagination or by putting on disguises. (See question 23.)

3. When they put on a disguise, it is usually a human form—any human form they want or any form we need to

see. Sometimes I wonder whether my guardian angel might not momentarily assume the form of my cat, when he crawls on my chest only when I am really sad.

4. Contrary to most greeting cards, angel books, and yard-sale statues, that human form does not usually have wings or a halo or a harp. Nor is it a fat, naked baby, a "cherub" (very different from the real cherubim, by the way, who are among the highest of the angels). These images, from human artists' imaginations, are only symbolic. Wings symbolize speed, halos of light symbolize wisdom or heavenly holiness, harps symbolize the beauty of spiritual harmony, and cherubic babies symbolize innocence—all of which angels really possess.

5. When angels appear, they don't all look alike since human beings don't all look alike. When angels put on human appearances, they select different ones, just as humans select different Halloween costumes. (But just as there are repeated favorite Halloween costumes—witches, ghosts, monsters—there are apparently repeated favorite human costumes for angels: tall, handsome, muscular young men seems to be a favorite, probably because it inspires confidence and fits a common human stereotype of the hero.)

Angels are each different by essence, so different that each angel is the sole member of its species. (See question 28.) There are no twin personalities among angels. So even when two angels look alike to humans, beneath the appearances they are radically different.

43 *Are angels beautiful?*

Absolutely. Beyond all human imagination. Because their inventor is beautiful. God is infinite Beauty and the inventor of all beauty in creatures. All the beautiful qualities in all of his art preexist more perfectly and beautifully in him, the Artist. The effect can't be greater than the cause. You can't give what you don't have. Now, angels are more Godlike than anything in nature. Therefore angels are more beautiful than anything in nature. (That's why people may have worshipped them as gods in times past; see question 50.)

But how can angels be beautiful if they have no bodies? Because spirits have greater potentialities than bodies, for good and evil, beauty and ugliness. Even human souls can be more beautiful than human bodies. That's why Mother Teresa is more beautiful than Madonna. So just as Satan is uglier than Stalin, Saint Michael the Archangel is more beautiful than Michael Jordan. (He's even got better moves.)

Only Mary's soul is as beautiful as an angel, because she is sinless.

The beauty of human souls "flows over" into the body, especially the face, and most especially the eyes. For the body—especially the eyes—expresses the soul, though very imperfectly. It partly reveals and partly conceals the soul. Therefore, it is appropriate that the bodily appearances of angels are awesomely beautiful.

44 *Do angels have a sense of humor?*

I think so. Because:

1. God does. That's obvious from a trip to a zoo. I dare you to stare at an aardvark or an ostrich and say God is wholly serious. And since angels are more like God than we are in other nonmaterial ways, they must have a pretty Godlike sense of humor—especially while they're guarding *us*.
2. The essence of humor is intellectual: the perception of paradox, or irony, or incongruity, or puns, or disproportion, or the unexpected. And since angels have very pow-

erful intellects, they are probably in hysterics half the time.

There are two other theories of humor that are popular among more cynical philosophers and psychologists. These two theories exclude angel humor. But both of these theories of humor are very low and gross and insulting to the high art of comedy. One says that humor is essentially a nervous reaction, a release of tension. That would mean there is only a difference in degree, not kind, between a laughing hyena and a laughing prophet. (Of course Jesus laughed. He was completely human. To find out why the Gospel writers did not mention this, read the end of G. K. Chesterton's *Orthodoxy*.) The other theory sees laughter as a social ploy, a power trip, or an expression of resentment, superiority, snobbery, or sneering. I can imagine Jesus yelling (at the money-changers in the Temple, for instance), but I can never imagine him sneering. And angels are not snobs either; if they were, they certainly would not guard and serve *us*.

For an explicit example of angel humor in Scripture, see Numbers 22: when a reluctant prophet made an ass of himself, an angel made his donkey into a prophet.

45 *Why did the medievals arrange angels into nine levels, or "choirs"?*

They began with their biblical database: nine names of ranks of angels occur throughout Scripture.

Then they reflected on the generic name "angel", meaning "messenger" (gofer).

Then they combined the two concepts and classified nine errands or tasks for angels:

The first three levels see and adore God directly:

1. The *seraphim*, the highest choir, comprehend God with maximum clarity, and therefore their love flames the hottest. ("Seraphim" means "the burning ones".) Lucifer ("Light-bearer") was once one of them. That's why he's still very powerful and dangerous.
2. The *cherubim* contemplate God too, but less in himself than in his providence, his wise plan for creatures. ("Cherubim" means "fullness of wisdom".)
3. The *thrones* contemplate God's power and judgments. (Thrones symbolize judicial, juridical power.)

The next three choirs fulfill God's providential plans for the universe, like middle management personnel:

4. The *dominations* or "dominions" (the name means "authority"), command the lesser angels below them.
5. The *virtues* receive their orders from the dominations and "run" the universe, so to speak, especially the heavenly bodies. ("Virtue" used to mean power, might, or energy.)
6. The *powers* serve the virtues by fighting against evil influences that oppose the virtues' providential plan.

The last three choirs directly order human affairs (they are like warriors):

7. The *principalities* care for earthly principalities, that is, cities and nations and kingdoms.
8. The *archangels* (such as Gabriel) carry God's important messages to man.
9. Ordinary *angels* are the "guardian angels", one for each individual.

The scheme is not official dogma, but it is a beautiful work of art, a reasonable work of philosophical speculation, an inspiring work of faith, and an enduring work of tradition.

1. No, and there are no male angels either. Angels have no bodies, therefore no biological gender.

2. But *masculinity* and *femininity* are broader than *male* and *female*. Masculinity and femininity can refer to personalities, souls, spirits. So angels could possibly be masculine and/or feminine, even though they could not possibly be male or female.

The idea that souls as well as bodies are masculine or feminine should not be surprising. Souls are not like ghosts haunting bodies as they haunt houses; there is a "psychosomatic unity" of soul and body, so that whatever deeply affects one affects the other too: pain, thought, death, love, age—and gender.

Pagan polytheism included goddesses as well as gods. If there is any truth behind this tradition (however perverted it became), and if the origin of these gods and goddesses is the (mistaken) worship of angels, then there may be feminine angels. C. S. Lewis, a paragon of Christian orthodoxy on almost all other issues, uses this pagan angelology in *Perelandra*, when he imagines the true Mars *and Venus*. Granted, the book is fiction, but all his other fictional symbols are consistent with Christianity, so it looks as if he meant this one to be, too. The passage is so evocative and archetypal that it begs to be quoted:

(In reading this passage, keep in mind that what Lewis—and all the world until the "sexual revolution"—calls "sex" meant then simply what we call "gender". Today "sex" means only *copulation*. What *he* calls "gender" is something for which we no longer have a word.)

> The Oyarsa [spirit] of Mars shone with cold and morning colours, a little metallic—pure, hard, and bracing. The Oyarsa of Venus glowed with a warm splendour, full of the suggestion of teeming vegetable life. . . .

Both the bodies were naked, and both were free from any sexual characteristics, either primary or secondary. That, one would have expected. But whence came this curious difference between them? He found that he could point to no single feature wherein the difference resided, yet it was impossible to ignore. One could try—Ransom has tried a hundred times—to put it into words. He has said that Malacandra [Mars] was like rhythm and Perelandra [Venus] like melody. He has said that Malacandra affected him like a quantitative, Perelandra like an accentual, metre. He thinks that the first held in his hand something like a spear, but the hands of the other were open, with the palms towards him. But I don't know that any of these attempts has helped me much. At all events what Ransom saw at that moment was the real meaning of gender. Everyone must sometimes have wondered why in nearly all tongues certain inanimate objects are masculine and others feminine. What is masculine about a mountain or feminine about certain trees? Ransom has cured me of believing that this is a purely morphological phenomenon, depending on the form of the word. Still less is gender an imaginative extension of sex. Our ancestors did not make mountains masculine because they projected male characteristics into them. The real process is the reverse. Gender is a reality, and a more fundamental reality than sex. Sex is, in fact, merely the adaption to organic life of a fundamental polarity which divides all created beings. Female sex is simply one of the things that have feminine gender; there are many others, and Masculine and Feminine meet us on planes of reality where male and female would be simply meaningless. Masculine is not attenuated male, nor feminine attenuated female. On the contrary, the male and female of organic creatures are rather faint and blurred reflections of masculine and feminine. Their reproductive functions, their differences in strength and size, partly exhibit, but partly also confuse and misrepresent, the real polarity. All this Ransom saw, as it were, with his own eyes. The two white creatures were sexless. But he of Malacandra was masculine (not male); she of Perelandra was feminine (not

> female). Malacandra seemed to him to have the look of one standing armed, at the ramparts of his own remote archaic world, in ceaseless vigilance, his eyes ever roaming the earthward horizon whence his danger came long ago. "A sailor's look," Ransom once said to me; "you know . . . eyes that are impregnated with distance." But the eyes of Perelandra opened, as it were, inward, as if they were the curtained gateway to a world of waves and murmurings and wandering airs, of life that rocked in winds and splashed on mossy stones and descended as the dew and arose sunward in thin-spun delicacy of mist. On Mars the very forests are of stone; in Venus the lands swim. For now he thought of them no more as Malacandra and Perelandra. He called them by their Tellurian [earthly] names. With deep wonder he thought to himself, "My eyes have seen Mars and Venus. I have seen Ares and Aphrodite." He asked them how they were known to the old poets of Tellus. . . . They told him [that] there is an environment of minds as well as of space. The universe is one—a spider's web wherein each mind lives along every line, a vast whispering gallery where . . . no secret can be rigorously kept. . . . In the very matter of our world, the traces of the celestial commonwealth are not quite lost. Memory passes through the womb and hovers in the air. The Muse is a real thing. A faint breath, as Virgil says, reaches even the late generations. Our mythology is based on a solider reality than we dream: but it is also at an almost infinite distance from that base. And when they told him this, Ransom at last understood why mythology was what it was—gleams of celestial strength and beauty falling on a jungle of filth and imbecility (199–202).

3. But the three biblical, Abrahamic, theistic religions—Judaism, Christianity, and Islam—all traditionally have not recognized any feminine angels, just as they have no goddesses and (until very recently among some "progressive" Protestant denominations) no priestesses. All the angels that appear in the Torah, the Bible, and the Qur'an are masculine. The same is true of angels in the lives of the saints.

There seem to be two reasons for this. First, the function of angels among men is to be God's messengers and God's warriors—two jobs that in nearly all societies, times, and places males rather than females perform. Perhaps they are just using the socially appropriate appearance or costume for that era.

A second reason is more than social. Perhaps the human appearance of angels is male for the same reason all the language and symbols for God are male in these three biblical religions—for angels are Godlike, closer to God by their nature than we are. God is never imaged as female in Judaism, Christianity, or Islam. Pagan, naturalistic, and pantheistic religions always have goddesses; theistic religions never do. The God of Jews, Christians, and Muslims is the Creator, transcendent to the universe, while the gods of paganism, naturalism, and pantheism are not. The doctrine of God literally creating the universe out of nothing rather than forming it out of any previously existing matter is unique to Judaism and the two religions that learned who God really is from the Jews. As a man is different from a woman and comes into her from without to impregnate her, so God is different from nature and comes in from without to impregnate her with miracles and human souls with salvation. The transcendence of God makes the masculine imagery necessary. God is not "Mother Earth", the womb of things. Things do not emerge from out of God's substance, like a web from a spider.

So angels, who come from heaven and are God's messengers, are closer to God than anything else is, and appear more like God than anything else does. They are portrayed as *hes* because God is *he*.

This is not male chauvinism, by the way. If anything, it's closer to female privilege. For all human souls are more like women than like men in relation to God. The Church is his *Bride*.

47 *Why do women see angels more often than men do?*

Probably because women are more intuitive, while men are more analytical. It is not politically correct to say that in our culture today, but every previous culture and time knew this "intuitively".

Of course the difference is a matter of degree, and relative, but it's real—just like the bodily differences between men and women. Remember the psychosomatic unity: bodies dimly reflect souls.

Angels are wholly intuitive, not analytical. (See questions 35–37.) They see the truth immediately rather than proceeding step by step, either deductively, from premise to conclusion in an argument, or inductively, from sense experience to general principles. Since women are a bit more like angels than men are in this way—since they are more on the angels' mental wavelength, so to speak—one would expect them to be more intuitively aware of angels and sensitive to their presence.

48 *Why are all the paintings of angels somehow unsuccessful?*

This is a remarkable fact. No matter how memorable and moving, no painting does more than *suggest* angels. None can actually depict them. Why?

1. Because you can't paint invisible things, spirits.
2. Because you can't capture supernatural things in natural terms, supracosmic things in cosmic categories. The most you can do is symbolize, suggest, point down an infinite corridor in a certain direction, and hope that the viewer will look *along* the clue rather than *at* it, like following a pointing finger.
3. Because the angel we unconsciously know is more true

and terrible and wonderful than any of the painted angels we consciously see, and this angel in the unconscious judges them as inadequate to it. How we ever got that standard in our mind to judge by is a further mystery. It's not conscious knowledge. We don't explicitly know what angels are, innately. But we do know what they're *not*—we say "not quite right" to all the paintings—and we couldn't do that unless we knew somehow, implicitly, what they *are*.

49 *Could angels be extraterrestrials?*

Angels are more extraterrestrial than extraterrestrials are; they are extra*cosmic*. Extraterrestrials come from other planets outside the earth; angels come not from another planet but from another universe, another order of creation entirely, one with no matter and therefore none of the space and time that are relative to matter.

Meeting a person of another nation and race is more remarkable, especially to a child, than meeting a person from another city. Meeting a person from another planet (an extraterrestrial) would be even more remarkable. Meeting a person from another universe is most remarkable of all.

Even though angels are extracosmic, they are still *persons*, of course. There can be nonhuman persons. A person is simply an *I*, a center of consciousness, some*one*, not just some*thing*, a subject and not just an object. A human being is a person who is a biological member of the human species, *homo sapiens*. Extraterrestrials (if there are any), angels, and God are persons in three very different ways, non-human persons.

(Confusion about the relationship between persons and humans can cause tremendous harm. Twice the U.S. Supreme

Court proved it badly needs philosophy lessons by missing the point that humans are a subdivision of persons rather than vice versa, that *all* humans are persons and therefore have the essential rights of persons. *Dred Scott* declared blacks less than full persons, thus justifying slavery and enforcing the return of runaway slaves as property, not persons. This took away the second fundamental right, liberty. A century later, *Roe vs. Wade* took away from unborn babies the first of a person's rights, the right to life. The philosophy on which this is based is essentially the same as the Nazis' in this sense: the state declares that it has the power to make a certain class of human beings non-persons [whether blacks, Jews, or unborn babies]. Besides being horrible morality, it is also bad logic. It treats "persons" as a smaller class than "humans". The existence of angels shows that it is a *larger* class.)

50 *Were the many gods worshipped by all ancient peoples (except the Jews) really angels? If angels are so wonderful, wouldn't it be natural for primitive people, who were in some ways like children, to be so overcome by awe as to worship them as gods if they ever saw them, especially in any undisguised form? Isn't it* unlikely *that on this issue alone the whole human race was totally wrong for 99 percent of all the time it has existed on earth, wrong about one of the most important things in life (superhuman beings, the supernatural), that they all thought these beings existed for no reason at all except pure fantasy and imagination with no basis whatsoever in reality? Isn't it likely, therefore, that the gods of ancient cultures were really angels?*

Maybe.

51 *How do you know if you are seeing an angel?*

1. If the angel is not wearing a human disguise, *you'll know*!

2. If he is wearing a human disguise, you won't know he's an angel if he doesn't want you to. Many humans "have entertained angels unawares" (Heb 13:2). Angels are smarter than we are. They probably don't make mistakes about their disguises.

3. Usually, angels disguised as humans reveal what they *are* by what they *do*: miracles. Jesus did the same. His supernatural acts revealed his supernatural identity. But his human nature was no disguise, as angels' human appearances are. Unlike angels, he was born and died, and he rose with a real human body.

52 *Are you sure angels have no wings? Why are they always painted with wings?*

Angels no more have wings than they have fins or gills. They are painted with wings to symbolize their job as heavenly messengers.

So we shouldn't take seriously the idea that angels get their wings after passing some tests, like Clarence in *It's a Wonderful Life*. Frank Capra was a great moviemaker, but he never claimed to be a great theologian.

53 *Why are angels painted with halos?*

Halos are made of light. Light is the primary material symbol for spirit, because of light's speed. Light is the fastest material, sensible thing in the universe.

C. S. Lewis explains the possible connection in *Out of the Silent Planet*:

> Body is movement. . . . If movement is faster, then that which moves is more nearly in two places at once . . . if you made it faster and faster, in the end the moving thing would be in all places at once. . . . Well, then, that is the thing at the top of all bodies—so fast that it is at rest, so truly body that it has ceased being body at all. . . .
>
> The swiftest thing that touches our senses is light. We do not truly see light, we only see slower things lit by it, so that for us light is on the edge—the last thing we know before things become too swift for us. But the body of an eldil [angel] is a movement swift as light; you may say its body is made of light, but not of that which is light for the eldil. His "light" is a swifter movement which for us is nothing at all; and what we call light is for him a thing like water, a visible thing, a thing he can touch and bathe in—even a dark thing when not illuminated by the swifter. And what we call firm things—flesh and earth—seem to him thinner, and harder to see, than our light, and more like clouds, and nearly nothing. To us the eldil is a thin, half-real body that can go through walls and rocks; to himself he goes through them because he is solid and firm and they are like cloud. And what is true light to him and fills the heaven, so that he will plunge into the rays of the sun to refresh himself from it, is to us the black nothing in the sky at night (94–95).

Another reason for halos is that light naturally symbolizes knowledge and wisdom, "enlightenment". We learn first through our senses, chiefly sight. "I see" means both "my eye perceives" and "my mind understands".

The halo surrounds the *head* because we naturally talk to people's heads, not their torsos. "The eyes are the windows of the soul." The head is heavenly.

54 *Do angels have a special connection with the sea?*

I know of no one who has ever claimed this in print, except Tolkien (see paragraph 3, below). But I strongly suspect there is something here. I "feel it in my bones". Here is my three-step justification for my gut feeling:

1. Though angels are pure spirits, they are creatures and messengers of the God who invented and loves the material world. (He murmured a satisfied "good, good!" after each day's work of creating more and more of it, according to Genesis.) So angels, being God*like*, may love matter too and may have special intimate relationships with some special parts of the material world. (Demons—evil angels—probably would not; they would be too proud to love lowly matter.)

2. So angels love matter, in general; but why the sea especially? Well, as almost everyone knows, angels have a special intimacy with another aspect of the material world: light. Angels often appear as "beings of light". Light is the first thing God created, and water is the second, according to Genesis. Now light and water are two of our primary material needs, two things we naturally desire. Light and water are also the two natural symbols of spirit. Scripture constantly uses both. Jesus heals the blind to symbolize his healing of the spiritually blind, and he calls the Holy Spirit "living water" (John 4:13–14; 7:37–39). "Living water" means, literally, *moving* water: rivers and seas, as distinct from lakes and ponds and pools and puddles. Moving water has a great effect on the human spirit, powerful magic. It is almost impossible to be an atheist if you grew up near the sea. Steel and concrete produce atheists, but not moving water. We intuitively know this and are drawn to the sea. Oceanfront property is always the most expensive and desirable. The sea is most people's favorite vacation spot. If angels especially love anything in the material world, it is probably stars and seas. Best of all, both: starlight reflected at sea.

3. Just what precisely is the connection between angels and the sea? Do angels raise and still storms? Are the waves their dance? Does the shimmer of water reflect their spirit to us? Who knows?

Perhaps Tolkien knows. In *The Silmarillion*, the angels (the Ainur) especially love the sea:

> But the . . . Ainur looked upon this habitation . . . , which the Elves call Arda, the Earth; and their hearts rejoiced in light, and their eyes beholding many colours were filled with gladness; but because of the roaring of the sea they felt a great unquiet. And they observed the winds and the air, and the matters of which Arda was made, of iron and stone and silver and gold and many substances; but of all these water they most greatly praised. And it is said . . . that in water there lives yet the echo of the Music of the Ainur more than in any substance else that is in this Earth; and many . . . hearken still unsated to the voices of the Sea, and yet know not for what they listen (19).

55 *Are angels especially connected with the stars?*

Yes, so much so that many of the ancients confused the two and worshipped the stars. But I think this error is more natural than the modern obtuseness of spirit that cannot even see the connection. I think the idolatrous error of worshipping the sun and the stars, wrong as it is, is not as wrong as being so insensitive to awe and worship that you are not even *tempted* to that idolatry. For, as Chesterton says, the gap between those who worship many gods and those who worship one, great as it is, is not as great as the gap between those who worship and those who do not.

The ancients often confused angels with stars in two ways.

The first confusion was as to what angels were made of. Some thought angels had bodies made of heavenly matter, more-than-earthly matter, such as the "quintessence" or "fifth essence" in medieval alchemy. (This was not one of the four essences or elements out of which all earthly things were supposedly made: earth, air, fire, and water.)

The other side of this same confusion was the unscientific idea that heavenly bodies (stars and planets) were changeless and immortal, like angels. Angels were brought down to the level of stars, and stars were raised to the level of angels.

The second confusion was the medieval idea that angels were required to *move* the heavenly bodies. They thought this because mere matter does not move itself, and the heavenly bodies move, and gravity was not yet formulated as a moving force. Aristotle had discovered only half the principle of inertia—that a body at rest remains at rest unless moved by another—but not the other half—that a body in motion remains in motion unless acted on by another. He did not know that moving bodies on earth slow down only because of atmospheric friction and that the bodies in the vacuum of outer space do not. Aristotle also believed that a vacuum was impossible. So, not having either gravity or inertia to explain the motion of the heavenly bodies in Aristotle's science, the ancients used angels.

The error may seem simply laughable to us moderns. Yet there is a kind of rightness to the error. Angels *ought* to have some special connection with the stars. We naturally and properly look *up* to see angels, not down. Though they do not literally come from outer space, or other galaxies, or other planets, or the clouds, any more than they come from holes in the ground, yet the former is the right symbol and the latter is a wrong one. There is something there, some truth to the connection, that we have not yet adequately understood and formulated, just as there seems to be also a special connection between angels and the sea, or angels and water.

56 *Do angels love? If not, how can they be good without loving? If so, how can they have emotions without having bodies or nerves?*

Yes, angels love. Contrary to the typically modern view, the essence of love is not an emotion but an act of will, goodwill. Will is spiritual, not physical. Pure spirits have will as well as intellect. But they do not have emotions, because emotion is psychosomatic; it is both spiritual *and physical.*

We too can love with the will even when we do not have loving emotions or feelings. We make this distinction toward *ourselves* quite easily, so we should be able to do it toward others too when necessary. We don't always have loving feelings toward ourselves. Sometimes we feel "I like myself", and sometimes we feel "I could kick myself", and sometimes we feel neither. But at all three times we can have goodwill toward ourselves; we can seek our own good. If we can do it to ourselves, we can do it to others too. Which is exactly what Scripture commands: "Love your neighbor *as yourself.*"

Physical emotions are moved by chemicals, nerve endings, weather, digestion, hormones, and a thousand other things in the body or the physical world. Animals can't love without physical emotion. Angels can't love *with* physical emotion. We can love with *or* without physical emotion. We have two kinds of love: animal (physical) love and angel (spiritual) love. If we couldn't love with physical emotion, we would be angels. If we couldn't love without physical emotion, we would be animals.

We can distinguish at least eight kinds of human love. Angels have only one of the eight. In the following list it is the last item, the only purely nonphysical love.

1. *Lust, or animal appetite.* Angels have no bodies or biological instincts so they have no animal appetites.

2. *Greed, or acquisitive desire.* Angels do not need anything like food or money or land. There is no way they can benefit

themselves by acquiring external goods. Therefore, they have no greed.

3. *"Puppy love", or infatuation.* This happens to human teenagers, but not angels. Angels are never teenagers, are never born, are never infants. They are fully adult as soon as they are created.

4. *Romance, or the Romeo–Juliet, Dante–Beatrice love.* This is a deeper, higher kind of infatuation. Angels don't fall in love this way either.

5. *Instinctive affection, or liking.* This is the kind of love based on comfortable familiarity, especially in a family. Angels have no families, so they don't have this kind of love either.

6. *Compassion, or sympathy, or pity.* This is a feeling-with or feeling-for another. Angels can understand human feelings, such as distress, but they do not have human feelings—they cannot become distressed themselves. They have a kind of cognitive sympathy.

7. *Friendship.* The Ancient Greeks and Romans regarded this as the highest form of love because it was the most spiritual and least physical. But (according to Aristotle) there are three forms of friendship, and angels can't have any one of the three. The first form is based on pleasure: having fun together. Angels don't go in for beer or football. The second form is based on need or utility: I want you for my friend because you have a car, or money, and I don't. Angels have no such needs. The third form is based on mutual respect, which angels have; but it requires equality between the two friends, and as we have seen (questions 28–30), there is no equality among angels. They can cooperate in a common work, like soldiers, but do not share common feelings or needs.

This may seem very disappointing, even cold. But remember, angels are aliens, different, radically other than humans. We can't make them after our desires. We didn't make them; God did. They are facts, not myths.

But angel love is not cold. They care for each other and for us—probably much more than any humans ever can. To see this, consider the eighth form of love:

8. *Charity* (*agape*), *or willing the good of the other.* Since this love comes from the will rather than the feelings, and since angels have wills, angels have this love. They are altruists. They will the good of other angels, whom they teach (see question 36), and the good of the humans whom they guard as "guardian angels" (see questions 60, 69, 81–83).

Although this love is not hot as animal passions are hot, it is not cold and uncaring either. Here is C. S. Lewis' portrayal of angel charity, in *Perelandra*:

> The faces surprised him very much. Nothing less like the "angel" of popular art could well be imagined. The rich variety, the hint of undeveloped possibilities, which make the interest of human faces, were entirely absent. One single, changeless expression—so clear that it hurt and dazzled him—was stamped on each and there was nothing else there at all. In that sense their faces were as "primitive," as unnatural, if you like, as those of archaic statues from Aegina. What this one thing was he could not be certain. He concluded in the end that it was charity. But it was terrifyingly different from the expression of human charity, which we always see either blossoming out of, or hastening to descend into, natural affection. Here there was no affection at all; no least lingering memory of it even at ten million years' distance, no germ from which it could spring in any future, however remote. Pure, spiritual, intellectual love shot from their faces like barbed lightning. It was so unlike the love we experience that its expression could easily be mistaken for ferocity (199–200).

57 *How many angels are there?*

1. More than five billion, for everyone has a guardian angel.

2. And since guardian angels are only the lowest of the nine "choirs", there must be many more angels than humans.

3. If there are also other intelligent species on other planets, and if they too have guardian angels, there would be many, many more.

Which is just what the Bible says. And the liturgy: "countless hosts of angels".

58 *Do angels have sex?*

Scandalous as it may sound to the worshippers of Venus, no.

Since they do not have bodies, or biological gender, or animal instincts or death, or (therefore) the need to reproduce, or families, they do not copulate.

However, according to traditional accounts, demons, or evil angels, sometimes copulate with humans, using the bodies they assume. (See question 24.) They are called "incubi" and "succubi". Demons hate nature (since it is God's creation and reflects his will) and love to pervert the natural order whenever they can. So they love to tempt us to "unnatural acts"—the more unnatural, the more they like it. Sex with evil spirits certainly seems to qualify, as much as sex with animals.

This may be what is referred to in Genesis 6:

> And it came to pass, when men began to multiply on the face of the earth, and daughters were born unto them, that the "sons of God" saw the daughters of men that they were fair; and they took them wives of all which they chose. And the Lord said, My spirit shall not always strive with man. . . .
>
> There were giants ("Nephilim") in the earth in those days, and also after that, when the sons of God came in unto the

> daughters of men, and they bare children to them, the same became mighty men which were of old, men of renown.
>
> And God saw that the wickedness of man was great in the earth (Gen 6:1–5 KJV).

The parents of the "Nephilim", the "giants in the earth", may have been incubi copulating with human women. The term *sons of God* is often a generic term for heavenly beings; they are not necessarily good, and among them is included Satan: cf. Job 1:6.

You see, there are a lot more things in the Bible than the nice stuff they taught you in catechism class.

59 *Are angels eternal?*

No. Only God is eternal. "Eternal" means (1) having no beginning and no end, and (2) having no past and no future. All reality is *present* to God at once. Angels are unlike God in these two ways:

1. Although angels will have no ending, they had a beginning. They were created.

2. They also are in spiritual time. They exercise one act of knowing or willing after another. But this purely spiritual time is not a *space*-time continuum, like material time. Its before-and-after is a series of quantum leaps, like strobe lights. (See question 40.)

Did angels begin when matter began, then, some twelve to eighteen billion years ago in the Big Bang? I think not. Their time is not the time of the material universe. They are not in physical time any more than they are in physical space, as matter is. They have to enter into this world from without. We cannot use the standards of time from this universe—either the revolutions of the "heavenly" bodies or the constant speed of light—to measure how old angels are.

Material time is a function of matter, is relative to matter. It does not exist *before* matter exists. Newton was wrong: there is no absolute and infinite time and space. Einstein is right: time and space are relative to matter in motion. They are generated by the motion of matter, somewhat as heat or scent is generated by an animal as it runs.

Medieval philosophers coined the word *aeveternity* for angel time. It is between eternity and time. Unlike eternity, it has a beginning and a before and after; but unlike the time of material creatures, it is not measured by matter or space, and it has no ending.

Because they are not in our kind of time continuum, angels do not get older, or wiser, or stupider, or better, or worse. At the moment of their creation they choose for or against God forever. They cannot change their fundamental choice. There is no excuse for their choice: no ignorance, no emotion, no temptation. They choose with the whole of their being. So demons can never repent their anti-God choice and therefore can never be saved.

60 *Do we each have a guardian angel? Are our guardian angels aware of us right now?*

Yes. There are twice as many persons as we can see in every place, every kitchen or classroom, every hospital or nursery. Only half are *human* persons. There's an angel standing next to each bag lady. Think of that next time you pass one by.

61 *Do angels see God and us at the same time?*

Yes. They have two faces, so to speak. Pope Saint Gregory the Great said that those angels God sends on errands to earth "always stand in the divine presence and see the face of the Father". Jesus said the same thing about the guardian angels of children (Mt 18:10): "See that you do not despise one of these little ones; for I tell you that in heaven their angels always behold the face of my Father who is in heaven."

62 *Can angels make us good?*

No. Only our free choices can make us good. No one, not even God, can make us good against our will. That would make free will unfree.

But angels can help, just as human friends can. They can be God's instruments. But we must use, or play, the instrument—just as we must accept and use human help.

Angels will occasionally perform miracles on matter, because matter is passive and unfree. But to force human wills miraculously would be to pervert the fundamental nature of the will as active and free.

63 *Can reading books about angels and thinking about angels make us good?*

People are thinking and reading a lot about angels lately—and that's good, because it's being realistic. Angels exist; that's the fundamental reason for thinking about them.

But that thinking isn't growing any halos on us. Why not?

First, because thinking about something is not becoming that something. You don't become an angel, or even like an angel, simply by thinking about angels.

Second, because *spirituality* is not the same as *goodness*. Getting closer to angels in your thought, being interested in pure spirits, is not necessarily getting any closer to goodness, that is, holiness, saintliness, morality.

There's no necessary connection between being a *spirit* and being *good*. The most evil beings that exist are pure spirits: demons. Matter, in contrast, is never evil. It's simply good, because God created it.

God created spirits too, and they are good *in their being* for the same reason that matter is. But spirits have wills and can choose between the *morally* good and the *morally* evil. Matter cannot.

If we need to be freed from materialism, thinking about angels will improve our *philosophy*. But only our own choices can improve our *character*.

64 *Do angels know our secret thoughts?*

No. They can't force themselves into our minds any more than they can force our wills. Neither good angels nor evil spirits can do this. Spirits don't work by force; matter does. Even God did not force the universe to exist; he simply *thought* and "spoke" it into existence.

But you can will to reveal your thoughts and your secrets to your guardian angel by talking to him, as you would talk (pray) to a human saint in heaven or a friend on earth.

A word to non-Catholic readers might be necessary here: praying to saints and angels does not mean *worshipping* or *adoring* them but simply talking to them and asking things from them, just as we do with each other on earth. "Pray" is a Middle English word for "please", as in "pray, tell me what's up", or "pass the mustard, I pray thee".

65 *How do angels affect our minds?*

As we affect each other: freely, by suggestion, not by force.

We can affect each other's minds and wills (though we cannot *force* them) by teaching, counseling, praising, blaming, exhorting, and commanding. We do this in bodily ways, unlike angels, but also by suggesting things to the imagination. (The imagination is the inner sense that makes images.) Angels can also suggest or inspire our imagination.

Now this is *not* direct mental telepathy. Angels teach each other by direct mental telepathy, but this is not the way they teach us. Rather, they "inspire" us; they *suggest* things to our imagination.

Evil spirits do the same. Demons tempt us in the same way as guardian angels help us.

Tempting is not forcing. A spirit or soul cannot be forced. There is no such thing as spiritual forcing. There is spiritual *power*, but it cannot force other spirits, because spirits are free; spirits have free will by their very essence. Even exorcists do not *push* demons out, they *pray* them out.

Jesus appealed to that principle of spirit being free, which the Pharisees had forgotten, when he criticized them for thinking that their souls were forcibly contaminated, made evil, by physical dirt. (See Mt 15:10–20.) Both defilement and purity come from within by free choice.

But we can *influence* (not compel) each other's choices through the mediating channels of imagination and emotion. So can angels. They can't put judgments in your mind or choices in your will, but they can put images in your imagination and feelings in your heart. (Feelings don't compel you either; your will can choose whether to follow your feelings or not.)

Intellect and will are spiritual. Emotions and imagination are quasi-physical, partly physical and partly spiritual. So they can be directly influenced from without, while spirit cannot be. (Spirit really *has* no "without".)

Sometimes we wonder how a certain emotion or image arose within us. From where did that feeling or picture come? Perhaps the missing factor is sometimes our guardian angel or tempting demon.

If anyone thinks this is unscientific rubbish, please reflect for a minute that the instruments designed for detecting visible, physical things are of course not going to reveal invisible, spiritual things even if they are there. You don't prove there are no ghosts by noting that they don't bat any baseballs.

66 *Can angels go through doors and walls?*

Yes, just like ghosts. Matter can't move through matter, but spirit can. Rocks don't move through rocks, but we can send our thought through rocks, over seas, or to the edge of the known universe with no resistance at all, because thought is spirit, not matter. Angels can move as easily as thought. (See the quotation in question 53).

67 *How do angels act on bodies, if angels are bodiless spirits?*

Angels do sometimes act on bodies—for example, stop speeding cars. *Some* of the many such stories that have been published lately are true, at least.

How do angels act on bodies? As corporations do: from a distance.

Think of a corporation in New York deciding the fate of a subsidiary, or an employee, or a client in Hawaii. Like a corporation, an angel is present wherever he makes a difference, wherever the body is on which he is acting. And at the same time he is present in heaven, because angels bilocate (questions 39 and 61).

A body is surrounded by space. But a spirit is not. Rather, a place is surrounded by the spirit. Not by his body, for he has none, but by his presence—for he's really there!—and by his power. He can really change things.

Just what that power is by which angels stop speeding cars, I don't know. It's not a physical power, since angels have no physical bodies, so it must be a power of mind and will. But its *effects* can be physical. This is not impossible, for it happens all the time within each of us when we think and will to move our arm, and then our arm moves. The gap between spirit and matter is bridged, somehow. It happens in us.

But if we can't explain even how we do it, we can hardly expect to explain how angels do it.

68 *Can angels cheer us up and make us happy?*

Angels can cheer us in all the ways they can affect us. And demons can oppress and depress us in the same ways.

Angels can even cheer us simply by being what they are: beautiful and inspiring objects of thought and wonder. Like the sea, or the stars, or the sunlight.

Angels can cheer us up, but they can't make us happy.

Cheeriness is an emotion, a temporary and subjective feeling. Happiness is a real and lasting state. True happiness is a state of *being*, not just *feeling*. We can be truly happy only insofar as we fulfill our being, complete our purpose, become what our Creator designed us to become, achieve success at life's most important job: not just being a good CEO or a

"An Angel with Halo"
S. Appolinare Nuovo, Ravenna, Italy

good teacher or a good pilot but being a good person, being *good.*

That's up to us. As William Law says, "If you will consult your heart in all honesty, you will know that there is only one reason why you are not even now a saint: you do not wholly want to be" (*A Serious Call to a Devout and Holy Life*).

Angels can't make choices for us. They are not *alternatives* but *additions*, not *escapes* but *expansions.* They are certainly not scapegoats. Never say "the devil made me do it". Eve tried that one, and it cut no ice at all with God (Gen 3:13), any more than Adam's pointing the finger at Eve.

69 *What are the different ways angels can affect us?*

1. As objects of thought, they can fascinate us and stimulate our curiosity and wonder.

2. As messengers from God, they can "deliver the good news", such as the news of Christ's coming (Lk 1:11–19, 26–38; 2:8–14).

3. As guardian angels, they can fight evil spirits that tempt us.

4. As guardian angels, they can miraculously protect us from physical harm (Ps 91:11–12). This is rare, however, and not to be counted on (especially when driving!).

5. As guardian angels, they can suggest things to our imagination or feeling. (See questions 65 and 68.)

70 *Do angels know the future?*

No, not unless God tells them. Only God knows the future: (1) because only God is all-knowing; and (2) because only the Author, the Creator, knows the whole play even before it's performed; and (3) because only God is entirely outside time, so that all things and events in time are present to him at once.

71 *Do angels ever raise or calm storms?*

It is in their power. But I doubt that they waste that power by playing with storms for no good, godly reason.

But just as Jesus stilled a storm for a good reason (Lk 8:22–25), angels can too. Of course they're only obedient soldiers; it's all up to General God. In all creation, only demons, and humans when we choose evil, ever do anything that isn't God's will.

72 *Can angels become cars?*

They can assume many forms, but they prefer natural, God-designed forms (like cats) to artificial forms like cars. Remind me never to ride with you if this strange question has ever crossed your mind.

Actually, a student really did ask it in my class.

73 *Do angels eat?*

They don't have to, since the bodies angels assume are not biological bodies made of organs and molecules that need food. They are only shaped like human bodies, as a lion costume is shaped like a lion but is not a lion.

However, since angels' human costumes are a lot more realistic than humans' angel costumes, part of their perfect disguise would be to eat whenever it was appropriate to do so.

The angel Raphael ate a fish in the story of Tobias (Tobit 6:1–5).

74 *Are the stories about rescues by angels true?*

Probably, like most stories, some are and some aren't. Only two groups of people would disagree with this answer: (1) the materialists, who claim to know that there are no spirits and thus believe *no* angel stories, and (2) people who even believe the *National Enquirer* and thus believe *all* angel stories.

75 *Can I expect ever to be rescued by an angel?*

No. Angel rescues are rare, like all supernatural interventions. You might experience it, but you shouldn't *expect* it. It's like a government agency that really works.

Moreover, angels don't rescue people who deliberately do foolish things. That principle is taught both by the current angel stories and by Scripture. (In Matthew 4:5–7 Satan *tempted* Jesus to throw himself down from the top of the temple like a ball for angels to catch.)

There was a movie (*Wings of Desire*) that turned this principle upside down. In this movie an angel told the hero to do just what the devil tempted Jesus to do: jump. Hollywood seems to love to make antibiblical movies today. For instance, in the "angel movie" *Defending Your Life*, the hero could go to heaven only if he had the "courage" to commit adultery. The religion of Hollywood.

76 *What do other religions say about angels?*

An adequate answer would take another book or three. There are such books, and you can easily find them.

Essentially, just about all religions teach that there exists something like angels: spirits superior to man but inferior to God. The three major Western religions, Judaism, Christianity, and Islam, all teach essentially the same thing (in their orthodox form) about angels. They also all teach essentially the same thing about the nature of God and about moral virtues and vices. Coincidence? I doubt it.

Other ancient religions in the West, which do not stem from God's revelation to Abraham and from the Bible, may have worshipped angels as gods. (See question 50.) In ancient Greek philosophy angels are spirits but not God's messengers, and they are not created by God. The idea of creation out of nothing is a distinctively Jewish (and subsequently Christian and Muslim) idea. These Greek spirits are superhuman intellects without bodies, and in Greek and medieval astronomy they are related in a special way to the planets, which they were thought to move in their orbits. (See question 55).

In the Bible, in contrast, angels are related not to planets or to the physical cosmos but to God (as his creatures), and to man (as our guardians), and to both as God's messengers to man.

The ancient pagan mind was *cosmocentric*; the medieval theistic mind (Jewish, Christian, and Muslim) was *theocentric*; and the post-Christian modem mind is *anthropocentric*, or humanistic. Thus the typically modern angel book is psychological: "your inner angel", you becoming an angel, that sort of stuff.

77 *Can we talk to angels?*

Why not? They're not hard of hearing. If we can talk to saints in heaven, why not to angels? And why would God send angels as messengers to us if we couldn't communicate with them? (See question 64.)

78 *Aren't angels irrelevant today? This is the age of man, isn't it?*

Yes, this is the age of man, of self-consciousness, of psychology. And therefore it is crucial to "know thyself" accurately today. The major heresies of our day are not about God but about man.

The two most destructive of these heresies—and the two most popular—are angelism, confusing man with an angel by denying his likeness to animals, and animalism, confusing man with an animal by denying his likeness to angels.

Man is the only being that is both angel and animal, both spirit and body. He is the lowest spirit and the highest body, the stupidest angel and the smartest animal, the low point of the hierarchy of minds and the high point of the hierarchy of bodies. (See question 19.)

More accurately stated, man is not both angel and animal because he is neither angel nor animal; he is *between* angels and animals, a unique rung on the cosmic ladder.

But whichever way you say it, man must know angels to know himself, just as he must know animals to know himself, for he must know what he is, and he must know what he is not.

79 *Are there ever "angels in the outfield"? Do angels ever account for the outcome of baseball games?*

Angels wouldn't do that. But demons might. Especially Red Sox demons.

How else has anyone ever been able to account for the supernaturally strange and torturous history of weird playoff losses? Did you catch a glimpse of horns when that little demon blew that ball through Buckner's legs with his bad breath? No, of course you didn't see him, but you saw the reverse miracle he performed in '86. Perhaps it was the same one that made Pesky hold the ball so Slaughter could score in '46 and blinded Larry Barnett's eye to Ed Armbrister blocking Carlton Fisk in '75 . . .

Sorry. We all have our infernal obsessions.

80 *Does each of us have his own angel?*

Yes, always at our side, "to light and guard, to rule and guide". They are our bodyguards and soulguards.

But not as servants or pets. If anything, we are like pets to them.

How can we be sure each of us has a guardian angel? Jesus says so (Mt 18:10), and the Church has always taught it.

But isn't this an old myth for children?

I'd rather rely on Jesus, the Bible, and the Church than on the kind of people who sneer at the teachings of these three as myths for children, thank you.

81 *What difference do guardian angels make?*

If it were not for guardian angels, we would be unprotected from forces that we are no match for: "principalities and powers" (Eph 6:12), evil spirits. We would be like sheep without shepherds surrounded by wolves. Or like hobbits without Rangers surrounded by Black Riders in *The Lord of the Rings.* If there were no guardian angels, Nazi Germany would be the *best* civilization in history.

82 *When do our guardian angels come to us to fight for us?*

They never leave us. When your guardian angel goes on an errand, he does not leave you any more than he leaves God. He bilocates or trilocates. Angels are not confined by space to only one place at a time, as bodies are.

Wherever you go, you take your angel. So before you go to any place, ask yourself whether it's a place that's fitting for an angel to go.

83 *Is the traditional picture of an angel whispering in one ear and a demon in the other true?*

Yes (symbolically, of course). There are two important truths in this picture.

First, angels' work is usually spiritual, not physical. Angels oppose demons, not cars or storms or poverty or lawyers. Angels *can* save us from physical harm and sometimes do, but every minute of every day they are helping us fight the greater spiritual battles.

Second, neither angels nor demons take away our free choice. Your guardian angel casts a vote for you, and a tempting demon casts a vote against you, and you cast the deciding vote.

PART FOUR

QUESTIONS ABOUT DEMONS

"God Testing Job's Faith by Allowing
the Devil to Destroy Job's Sheep"
Bibliothèque Nationale, Paris

You bet your eternal life they do.

Here is a logical argument for the existence of demons:

If angels are persons (selves) they have intellects and wills. If they have wills, they can choose between good and evil. If they can choose between good and evil, they can choose evil. If they choose evil, they become evil. So if there are good spirits, there can be evil spirits.

Philosophical reasoning alone can establish the *possibility* of demons (evil spirits), just as it can establish the possibility of angels. But just as reason alone cannot prove that God freely chose to create actual angels, it cannot prove that some of these angels freely chose evil. Both God's choice and theirs are free, not necessary.

We know from philosophical reason that demons *can* exist, but we know from divine revelation (Bible and Church) that demons *do* exist. A small number of people also know them from experience. Ask any exorcist. (Yes, they really exist too. And not just in Hollywood films.)

We do not know much about demons from revelation. The horns and hoofs, the tights and tails, the grotesque faces and fantastic tales, come from another, merely human, source. Even scriptural imagery is only *imagery*: the devil is said to be "*like* a roaring lion, roaming about seeking someone to devour".

But the existence of demons is *de fide*, defined dogma. The Fourth Lateran Council declared that "Satan and the other devils are (1) by nature spirits . . . (2) created by God, (3) and so originally good, (4) but fell into sin (5) of their own free will" and that they are (6) "eternally damned". The new *Catechism* repeats this (391–95).

The Church does not have the authority to alter or subtract from her "deposit of faith" or "sacred tradition" because she is not its author, only its prophet. She interprets and explains it and increasingly develops its inner meaning and outer applications, but she does not edit it or change it, especially not to conform to current secular fashions. By still insisting on the unfashionable belief in evil spirits, the Church is not trying to turn the clock back two hundred years. Her program is to bring us back two thousand years to meet the One who founded her and taught her first apostles, and through them all their successors. She can teach only what she has been taught. And her Lord has taught that there are demons. If he had taught that there are purple space ships, she would be faithfully repeating it now, for she would know that there would in fact *be* purple space ships somewhere.

85 *Isn't it psychologically unhealthy to believe in demons? Isn't this a regression to medieval fear, superstition, and witch-hunting?*

If wild animals exist, is it unhealthy to believe they exist? Isn't it much more unhealthy to pretend they don't?

You can't find out whether or not a thing exists simply by observing the psychological effects that belief in that thing sometimes has in some people.

There are usually two possible errors about anything. Satan is equally pleased by our overestimating him *and* our underestimating him—as the commander of an enemy army in wartime would be equally pleased if your side greatly overestimated his strength and shook with superstitious fear when there was "nothing to fear but fear itself", *or* if you greatly underestimated his strength, or even stopped believing in his very existence. Either mistake will certainly lose battles and possibly lose the war. If our ancestors tended to the mistake of overemphasizing the devil (and this was indeed unhealthy), we tend to the opposite mistake: forgetting that life is spiritual warfare, that there *is* an enemy, that "we wrestle not against flesh and blood but against principalities and powers of wickedness in high places" (Eph 6).

Demons and Satan and hell are part of the package deal of divine revelation. The thing as a whole is our data, dumped into our laps, not arrived at as the conclusion of our philosophical debates. If you say you believe in the rest of the package, as revealed in the Bible and the creeds, but not demons, then you have set yourself up as the judge and corrector of divine revelation rather than letting it judge and correct you. You are treating God as your student, not your Teacher.

Once you lighten the load by throwing overboard one part of the cargo that your ship was ordered to deliver, you have turned yourself from servant into master, and you will certainly throw overboard more, and more important, cargo the next time the ship seems to be in trouble. That is why part of the "package deal" is the guarantee that this ship, the Church, will never, never sink. The gates of hell will not prevail against her! So how could the mere *doctrine* of hell and devils be too heavy for her to carry without sinking?

86 *What difference does belief in demons make?*

If demons aren't real, then either all angels are good or there are no angels at all.

We've already seen what difference it makes if no angels exist. (See question 4.) And if there are no demons but only good angels, then (to put it crudely) the deck is stacked, we can relax, we can't lose, we can be easy optimists, because we have only friends in high places and no enemies.

If demons are real, spiritual warfare is real, and "to the victor belong the spoils": your soul. The difference it makes when you know you are at war, when you know those are real, live bullets whistling past you, is the difference between sleeping and walking, the difference between a hot tub and a hot seat. On a battlefield, a matter of life or death appears as exactly what it is: a matter of life or death. And everything else—even the IRS or your in-laws or your sexual "needs"—appears as exactly what it is: *not* a matter of life or death.

87 *What can demons do?*

1. As objects of thought, they can inspire fear.

2. They can pervert God's revelations or deceive us with false revelations. Even the devil can appear "as an angel of light" (2 Cor 11:14).

3. They can tempt us through our imagination or feeling.

4. Occasionally they can even move matter supernaturally. This is even rarer than angelic supernatural intervention, but it happens.

5. But demons can *possess* us only if we choose to invite them in. (See question 88).

88 *Should we fear the devil and demon possession?*

Don't ask me, ask Jesus. He says, "I tell you, my friends, do not fear those who kill the body and after that have no more that they can do. But I will warn you whom to fear: fear him who, after he has killed, has power to cast into hell; yes, I tell you, fear him!" (Lk 12:4–5).

There are three levels of demonic influence on men: (1) temptation, (2) oppression, and (3) possession. Temptation comes to everyone. Oppression, in the form of great sorrow of spirit or great external tragedies, happens to many. Possession is rare and happens only to those who are asking for trouble by violating God's essential safety precautions such as his severe prohibition against the occult: "There shall not be found among you any one who burns his son or his daughter as an offering, any one who practices divination, a soothsayer, or an augur, or a sorcerer, or a charmer, or a medium, or a wizard, or a necromancer. For whoever does these things is an abomination to the Lord" (Dt 18:11–12). The same evil spirits who inspire human sacrifice inspire these other activities. Serious fortune-telling, seances, or ouija boards are linked to the same demonic causes as sacrificing one's children. All Hollywood hype aside, the real demon possession behind *The Exorcist* film began with playing a ouija board. That is asking for trouble in a big way, freely opening the door of your soul to—you know not what. That's the only way any spirit, evil *or* good, can enter your soul: by your free choice.

When Israel entered the Promised Land, the Canaanites were worshipping demon spirits: Astarte (Ashtaroth) and Moloch. The valley of Gehenna, or Ge Hinom, outside Jerusalem, was the place of human sacrifice of children to these demons. The Jews thought this place so evil that they would not live there but only burned their garbage there, day and night. They didn't have matches, so the fire had to be kept lit and never be allowed to die out. This was the image Jesus used for hell: Gehenna.

Spirits never die. Moloch still demands human sacrifice, four thousand every day in America alone. The demon spirit behind the smoke that rose from Ge Hinom is quite possibly the same spirit behind the smoke that rises from the chimneys of abortion mills today and the smoke that rose from the chimneys of Auschwitz fifty years ago and from the pyramids of Mexico City almost five hundred years ago.

I certainly do not mean that all Canaanites, Aztecs, Nazis, or abortionists are, in the strict sense, demon-possessed. But a demon can corrupt a national consciousness, just as an angel (a "throne"—see question 32) can inspire and care for a nation.

89 *How did angels fall and become demons?*

Angels were created with free will and tested in heaven, as we were on earth (in the Garden of Eden). Some chose to love and serve God. Others chose to rebel.

Scripture describes this as "war in heaven" (Rev 12:7). Demons were then expelled from heaven forever (12:8). Now, earth is the only place we know of where there is spiritual warfare (12:9), war between good and evil. Heaven has no evil, hell has no good, and mere matter—the rest of the created universe as far as we know—has neither moral good nor moral evil. Only here on earth is there war, both on external battlefields and on the internal battlefields of human hearts—which is the obvious source of all external wars. All this began when the demons first rebelled.

Probably, this rebellion was a single choice made at the moment of the angels' creation, made with their whole mind and free will, which they could never take back because there was no ignorance, no temptation, no excuse, and no part of the self holding back.

The "war in heaven" that erupted when Lucifer ("Lightbearer") fell and became Satan ("the Accuser") is described in the Bible in two passages:

> Now war arose in heaven, Michael [whose name means "Who Is like God?" and thus shows the lie of Satan's pride] and his angels fighting against the dragon [Satan]; and the dragon and

"Fall of the Rebel Angels"
Très Riches Heures du Duc de Berry (15th cent.)
Limbourg Brothers
Musée Condé, Chantilly, France

> his angels fought, but they were defeated and there was no longer any place for them in heaven. And the great dragon was thrown down, that ancient serpent, who is called the Devil and Satan, the deceiver of the whole world—he was thrown down to the earth, and his angels were thrown down with him.
>
> —Rev 12:7–9

> How are you fallen from heaven, O Day Star ["Lucifer"], son of Dawn!
> How are you cut down to the ground, you who laid the nations low!
> You said in your heart, "I will ascend to heaven;
> above the stars of God I will set my throne on high;
> I will sit on the mount of assembly in the far north;
> I will ascend above the heights of the clouds,
> I will make myself like the Most High."
> But you are brought down to Sheol, to the depths of the Pit.
>
> —Is 14:12–15

Lucifer, Light-bearer, was the greatest of all creatures, highest angel, Top Guy next to God—and *he* rebelled and invented evil. Many of the angels (one third of them, according to an old tradition) rebelled with him.

Their war was a real war. It is not symbolic language. It was not a physical war, because angels do not have physical bodies, but it was a real war, a war of wills, of minds, like a war between paralyzed telepaths. The military symbols we use for it are not too strong but too weak. So are any alternative physical symbols, whether clashing swords or clashing musics (Tolkien, in *The Silmarillion*), or clashing lights, like fiery, fighting strobes, or dueling lightnings. The war was more passionate, intense, and terrifying than any physical war or any physical symbol can convey.

The Qur'an tells the story of Satan's rebellion in this way:

> Then verily We [Allah] shall narrate unto them [the event] with knowledge, for verily We were not absent [when it came

> to pass]. . . . And We created you [mankind], then fashioned you, then told the angels: Fall ye prostrate before Adam! And they fell prostrate, all save Iblis [Satan], who was not of those who make prostration. He [Allah] said: What hindered thee that thou didst not fall prostrate when I bade thee? [Iblis] said: I am better than him. Thou createdst me of fire while him Thou didst create of mud. He [Allah] said: Then go down hence! It is not for thee to show pride here, so go forth! Lo, thou are of these degraded (Surah VII, 7–13).

This account puts only a slightly different spin on an ancient Jewish tradition in which God revealed to the angels his plan to create man, and when he commanded them to bow before this less intelligent creature bound to an animal body, some refused their primary duty of obedience, or (as Muslims call it) *islam*. Milton's version in *Paradise Lost* has Satan say: "Better to reign in Hell than serve in Heaven."

The Christian version "works" even better: God revealed to the angels his plan not only to create man but to incarnate himself in man, in Jesus. Satan and the other "dignified" angels refused to accept this "undignified" plan and bow to a God of flesh and blood. In all three versions, the first sin is pride, *Non serviam*, "I will not serve."

90 *When did this angelic fall happen?*

Probably at the moment of their creation, or (to be more exact) at the first moment after it. But these angelic "moments" are not part of our time, which is measured by matter. It is a different *kind* of time (see question 59), not measured by suns or clocks.

Matter was probably created twelve to eighteen billion years ago in the "Big Bang". Were angelic spirits also created then? No, for that "then" is measured by matter. We simply do not have the measuring stick to answer this question. There are in our universe no standards, no graphs on which to calibrate angel time.

91 *Explain the motivation for Satan's fall. Why would a wholly good angel choose to become a devil?*

Well, if it comes to that, why would a wholly good man, innocent and fresh from the creating hand of God, choose to become a sinner? What the Bible calls "the mystery of iniquity" is just that: a mystery, not perfectly transparent to reason. Evil is not rational; it is irrational.

How did Satan fall? Who tempted him? No one. The buck stops completely there. What motivated him? Simply his own pride. He resented being Number Two, inferior to God.

Did he know that that pride would make him miserable? Probably. Sin is not rational. Ultimately, there is never any good reason for any sin. Something less than reason, something that ought to be obeying reason, rose up and rebelled against reason.

All sin, whether of angels or of men, is irrational. It exchanges happiness for misery, heavenliness for hellishness. To the question What man would ever be insane enough to choose freely the hell of selfishness and pride over the heavenly joy and Edenic paradise of self-sacrificial love? the answer is: look in the mirror.

92 *How do demons tempt us?*

First, demons tempt us by arousing our selfish passions for false gods, by placing before our imagination false pictures of happiness that supposedly would come our way by worshipping and serving ourselves or something less than ourselves, something in our world. The fundamental temptation is to disobey the First and greatest Commandment: to love God with our whole heart.

This temptation can happen in three ways, corresponding to "the world, the flesh, and the devil" as the three traditional sources of temptation:

1. "The world" means *greed* for the things of the world, such as money, fame, and power.
2. "The flesh" means fallen human nature and *lust* (physical or spiritual) for selfish self-gratification, whether sexual or other.
3. "The devil" means sins that come from Satan's fall: spiritual sins, especially *pride* (playing God), as well as envy, jealousy, and resentment.

Satan's second strategy is to confuse us, to dim our lights—for instance, by convincing us that truth is negotiable, "nuanced", not ever plain and simple and certain and crude and obvious; that God's revelation is a dark puzzle for theologians, not a bright lamp for travelers.

Then, once we've put our minds first and God's second, Satan convinces us of the "dimwit" principle that sin is fun, that a little evil is good for us.

The two main parts of this satanic strategy—arousing selfish passions (biological or psychological) and dimming the light of reason—reinforce each other. Passion clouds reason, and clouded reason fails to enlighten passion.

93 *What are some specific ways devils tempt and deceive us, especially today? Please give me some detailed, specific, practical advice.*

Read C. S. Lewis' *Screwtape Letters.* And Appendix B of this book, which is an extension and an updating of Lewis' idea.

94 *Is exorcism for real? Do exorcists really cast out demons?*

Only God can cast out demons, but he uses human instruments (exorcists). Exorcism is one of the Church's official and traditional ministries. It is very rare, but it is very real.

The movie *The Exorcist* (I) was based on a true case history, with names, cities, genders, and some details changed. The head didn't really turn 360 degrees around. But the sounds you heard from Linda Blair's throat were a tape recording of the voice of a demon-possessed boy during an actual exorcism. William Peter Blatty, the author of the book, did extensive and careful research for it. Exorcism happens.

But exorcism is rare, like all supernatural interventions. The Catholic Church will not bring in an exorcist until all natural explanations and treatments have been considered and tried and have failed, just as she will not claim a miracle has happened (for example, at Lourdes or Fatima) until all natural explanations, both physical and psychological, are exhausted by careful investigation.

The Church has always had exorcists, ever since Christ and his apostles. That was a part of their ministry and proof that it was not just human: "If I cast out demons by the finger of God, then the kingdom of God has come upon you" (Lk 11:20). The Church is only the continuation of the work of Christ—all of it, including this.

95 *Can demons possess cats? What about computers?*

Cats need no demons; they are already completely evil.

(That was a cheap shot. Apologies to furry innocent felines.)

Demons want to possess human souls, block their eternal salvation, and feast on them in hell. They don't want cats; they want you.

Stories of witches using cats as "familiar spirits" are probably only legendary. However, demons can manipulate any material vehicles on occasion, including animals.

Computers, now, are another story. No apologies to them.

96 *Could the false gods or idols that ancient peoples worshipped have been demons?*

Some of them. Scripture strongly suggests this throughout the Old Testament history of God patiently training his people to worship him alone as they fell into idol worship time after time. Other passages suggest that the gods of the pagans are mere pieces of wood and stone (Ps 115:6). The two sets of passages do not contradict each other. *Some* of the "gods" of the pagans were probably only stones, and some were demons.

Both bad possibilities are still open to anyone who will not worship the true God: false idols of money, sex, and power or demons of hatred, resentment, and arrogance.

Read the story of the Aztec worship of the demon-god who demanded assembly-line human sacrifice (for example, Warren H. Carroll's *Our Lady of Guadalupe and the Conquest of Darkness*) or look at the pictures of Auschwitz or of dismembered or saline-shriveled unborn babies and tell me these are only human evil.

97 *Is all "spiritual warfare" supernatural? Are demons our only enemies?*

No. Spiritual warfare is the battle between Good and Evil in all forms. The battleground is human souls. As Solzhenitsyn says, the line that divides Good and Evil runs not between nations or parties or physical armies but right down the middle of every human soul.

Not all evil comes directly from demons; not all evil is supernatural. Most is natural and comes from the world or the flesh. (See question 92.) But even these sources of evil are devil-directed, used, or choreographed. Our natural battles are surrounded by a supernatural battle.

We are surrounded by two invisible armies, and the army of the loyal angels is greater and stronger than the army of rebel angels. We desperately need to recapture this vision today—first of all, simply because it is true, it is there. The vision includes two essential truths: first, the "bad news" that "our struggle is not against flesh and blood but against principalities and powers"; second, the "good news" that Good is vastly stronger than Evil. We need to pray, like Elisha, that God will open our eyes to see what is really there. The story I refer to gives me goose bumps every time I read it:

> So he [the King of Syria] sent there horses and chariots and a great army; and they came by night, and surrounded the city. When the servant of the man of God [Elisha] rose early in the morning and went out, behold, an army with horses and chariots was round about the city. And the servant said, "Alas, my master! What shall we do?" He said, "Fear not, for those who are with us are more than those who are with them." Then Elisha prayed, and said, "O Lord, I pray thee, open his eyes that he may see." So the Lord opened the eyes of the young man, and he saw, and behold, the mountain was full of horses and chariots of fire round about Elisha (2 Kings 6:14–17).

They are there. God did not put a vision *into* the man's eyes; he simply opened the man's eyes so he could see what was really there. As we see the forces of darkness increasingly settle on America like a cloud, we must also see God's fiery angel army surrounding them, so that we will fight with confidence—and with victory.

98 *What can I do to help fight this spiritual war?*

1. Be aware of it. Believe it.

2. Use the weapons God has provided. Scripture calls them "the whole armor of God" and lists them in Ephesians 6:10–18.

3. Pray daily.

99 *How can we mere men get supernatural help to fight supernatural foes? How should we pray?*

1. Pray to your guardian angel, the prayer every child used to know:

> Angel of God, my guardian dear,
> To whom God's love commits me here,
> Ever this day be at my side,
> To light and guard, to rule and guide.

2. Pray to Saint Michael the Archangel the prayer Pope Leo XIII was given when, near the end of the nineteenth century, he had a prophetic vision of the coming century of sorrow and war. In this vision God gave the devil the choice of one century in which to do his worst work, and the devil chose the twentieth. So the Pope was given a warrior's prayer for the Church in the coming century:

Saint Michael Archangel, defend us in battle!
Be our protection against the wickedness
    and snares of the devil.
May God rebuke him, we humbly pray;
And do thou, O Prince of the heavenly host,
    by the power of God,
Thrust into hell Satan and all the evil spirits
Who roam through the world seeking the ruin of souls.

3. Pray to Mary, the Second Eve, the Lady who conquered the serpent who seduced the first Eve (Gen 3:15). She conquered that serpent two thousand years ago (see Rev 12), and again in Mexico in 1519, and again in Germany in 1945, and again in Russia in 1989, and she can do the same in the nation pious Muslims now call "the great Satan", a civilization that spills the human blood from millions of tiny victims every year into the hungry mouth of Moloch. Only the Queen of Angels and her heavenly army can defeat this evil angel of death and change our culture from a "culture of death" into a culture of life and light and love.

4. Pray to the Lord of all, to complete the mop-up operation he is currently carrying on as the extension of his D-Day invasion two thousand years ago into the enemy-occupied territory of this world. The good news is that the rightful Commander has landed, under cover, is still present, invisibly, in his Church, in the souls of his faithful people, and in the Eucharist, and he will remove his disguise, reveal himself in all his glory, and defeat the devil so definitively that he will never rise again—in his good time, at the end of time.

Until then, he has given us our marching orders. Let there be no sleeping on our watch. The night is far spent; the morning is about to break.

100 *Can angels help us to win this war?*

Yes.

❦ ❦ ❦

Rank on rank the host of Heaven
spreads its vanguard on the way,
As the Light of Light descendeth
from the realms of endless day,
That the powers of Hell may vanish
As the darkness clears away.

—Cherubic Hymn
"Let All Mortal Flesh Keep Silence"
Liturgy of Saint James

APPENDIX A
A Short Course in Angelistic Philosophy

Many of the mistakes in the history of philosophy come from confusing men with angels. Here are some of these "angelistic" errors, in eight branches of philosophy.

1. ANGELISTIC METAPHYSICS

Metaphysics is that division of philosophy which studies being, or reality, that is, all reality, reality as such. Two forms of angelism in metaphysics are: (a) spiritualism, or the denial of the *reality* of matter; and (b) gnosticism, or Manicheism, the denial of the *goodness* of matter.

a. Spiritualism is found in most forms of Hinduism and Buddhism, Christian Science, New Age philosophy, and the philosophical systems of Leibnitz and Berkeley.

It is angelistic, of course, because angels have no matter.

Pantheism—the teaching that all ("pan") is God ("theos") and God is all—is usually a form of spiritualism. For if God is spirit and all is God, then all is spirit.

Pantheism is only about 18 billion years behind the times. It has not yet heard the good news that God created matter.

b. Gnosticism and Manicheism, the denial of the *goodness* of matter, are found today in many currently fashionable "spiritualities" whose goal is not freedom from *sin* but freedom from matter and externality.

This philosophy can be practiced perfectly only in hell, where the ego will have nothing external to itself and will be left to feed on itself alone forever. (Hell's fires, I think, are symbols, not literal realities—symbols of something more terrible than literal fire: the soul-destroying fire of sheer egotism and loneliness.)

Like pantheism, Gnosticism is behind the times. It has not yet heard the good news that when God created matter, he declared it to be good.

2. ANGELISTIC EPISTEMOLOGY

Epistemology is that division of philosophy which studies knowledge and how we know. Three prominent forms of angelism in epistemology are:

a. Cartesian Rationalism, which roots all certainty in the purely mental "I think, therefore I am" instead of humbly beginning by accepting sense experience of the material world. Descartes trusts his inner angel (intellect) but not his inner animal (senses).

b. Lockean Empiricism, which is also angelistic, even though it relies on sense experience instead of abstract reason. For Locke's fundamental error, right at the beginning of his system, is an angelistic one: he "thingifies" ideas. He says that the first and immediate object of thinking is an idea, not a real thing.

This logically leads to skepticism (the denial that we can ever have certain knowledge), as Locke's successor, Hume, saw. For if all I can directly know is my own ideas and not real beings, then I can never check whether these two match. It's like seeing only photographs or television images. I'm stuck inside my own mind (even if, as the empiricist teaches, that mind is dependent on the senses).

c. Kantian Idealism, which says that the mind imposes its innate a priori categories on experience rather than deriving them from experience. Kant calls this "the Copernican Revolution in philosophy": reversing the positions of knowing mind and known object, as Copernicus reversed the positions of earth and sun. According to Kant, objects conform to the mind rather than mind conforming to objects. Mind rules rather than is ruled.

Actually, this is worse than confusing human minds with angels: it is confusing human minds with God!

Descartes is the father of modern Rationalism, Locke of Empiricism, and Kant of Idealism: the three major schools of classically modern philosophy. All three, in different ways, are forms of the fallacy of angelism.

3. ANGELISTIC RELIGION

Angelistic religion is the confusion of religion's proper end, *sanctity* (freedom from *sin*), with *spirituality* (freedom from *matter*).

God did not do this. He created matter, incarnated himself in matter, redeemed matter, and continues to work through matter: a visible Church and material sacraments. To say that the material act of having water poured upon your head or the act of opening your mouth and eating what looks like a piece of bread could not possibly be God-instituted ways to eternal life is to be more "angelistic" than God.

There is nothing necessarily good about being more "spiritual" and less material. The devil is a pure spirit. God, on the other hand, has a body (ever since the Incarnation and Ascension).

How often have you heard the sentiment that "religion shouldn't worry about external forms, only the inner spirit"? That may be "religion", but it is not Christianity. If that sentiment were true, God never would have sent his Son into a pain-filled material world to suffer a bloody death, and we would have been left with only our own "inner spirits" and good intentions. Not enough! Not enough to save us from a fate worse than death.

4. ANGELISTIC ETHICS

a. The most common form of this mistake is the (Kantian) idea that the only thing that matters is your inner, spiritual intention. As long as you are sincere, it's O.K. The external, material deed does not have moral value.

That is a cruel joke to tell to the victims of the Holocaust. Hitler was quite sincere. It is also an ethic we do not want our surgeon to believe in. Doing the wrong thing for the right reason (spiritual intention) is still doing the wrong thing. Both the material thing *and* the spiritual intention count.

b. A second form of angelistic ethics is the (Platonic). doctrine that all you need is education; that evil is only moral ignorance (ignorance of the truth that morality is always good for you, always profitable, always makes you happy). Plato argues that because evil is ignorance, virtue is knowledge: to *know* the good is always to *choose* the good and to *be* good. We know from our experience that however reasonable this sounds, it is simply not true: many times, we knew darn well what we should do, and yet did not do it.

Aristotle, more realistically, teaches that we must not only know the good but also practice habits of doing it, especially by controlling our selfish passions. Only "intellectual virtues" (intelligence, wisdom, science) can be taught; moral virtues, such as justice, courage, self-control, and generosity, must be acquired by repeated practice and building up habits of character—something angels do not need to do.

Plato's error is very popular today, because it means we need not ever be "judgmental"; it means that whenever we see people doing something wicked, we can excuse them by saying that they are just ignorant. On the other hand, we often expect educated people to be more ethical than the uneducated. If anything, statistics show the opposite! For instance, a study of the Nazi concentration camps showed that the cruelest torturers were the most highly educated. Intelligence doesn't automatically make you good. The most brilliant mind in existence, next to God, was Lucifer before his fall.

5. ANGELISTIC ANTHROPOLOGY

What is it to be a human being? Plato's (angelistic) answer is: to be a soul. The self *is* the soul. This is noble-sounding, but false. Noble-sounding because if you believe it you will more easily be indifferent to bodily harm. (If you are only a soul, then what happens to your body is like what happens to your clothes.). But it is false because your body is not like your clothes: it is part of your very self. You can take your clothes off, you can't take your body off.

Plato also believed in reincarnation. This belief fits an "angelistic" anthropology because if you get reincarnated into different bodies, the "you" common to all bodies is not a body at all, only a soul; you just change motels when you die. In that case, death doesn't matter much; neither does birth. Another consequence is that the Christian doctrine of the resurrection of the body is a threat, not a promise. For if you believe in reincarnation, your goal is to be freed from all bodies, which are like prisons, and become a pure spirit, like an angel; to escape from this round of motels and get home.

Another angelistic heresy in anthropology is the idea that souls are sexless, that when we go inward from body to soul we leave sexuality behind. This is angelism because it confuses human souls, which are the animating principles of sexually differentiated bodies, with angelic pure spirits, which are indifferent to bodies and to sexuality.

If you accept the two premises that (a) sexuality is essential and intrinsic to the body, and that (b) the body is not a mere extra, like clothes, but the body is the very thing that the soul is the soul *of*, the life of, the form of; then (c) it logically follows that sex is in souls as well as in bodies, and that there is such a thing as a typically masculine and feminine mind and feelings. Feminity and masculinity are more complex and spiritual things than simply sex-organ structure and hormones. They have much to do with our personalities.

Finally—a third "angelistic" idea in anthropology—many people (not all) who are fascinated with OBEs (out-of-body experiences) and ESP (extrasensory perception) are "angelists" who yearn for bodilessness. OBEs and ESP do really *happen*, but they are not *natural* or normal for us "rational animals".

6. ANGELISTIC POLITICS

One form of angelistic politics is utopian schemes that ignore the history of human passions, prejudices, and sins. Another is anarchism, the desire to be totally free from government. The Federalist Papers (no. 51) say: "If men were angels, no government would be necessary." Embodied man is by nature a political animal.

The "social contract theory" of politics is also angelistic (to a lesser degree than anarchism), because it maintains that the state is not natural but artificial, that man is not by nature a political animal. It also tends to see men as atomistic individuals (like angels), not as essentially rooted and embedded in families and traditions. Indeed, this is a tendency in almost all modern political philosophies. Totalitarianism is simply the flip side of this angelistic individualism: it melds the uprooted individuals into an ant-heap. Neither individualism nor totalitarian collectivism sees that it is our essence to be embodied in roots, families, traditions, heredity, and history.

Both the Left and the Right can be angelistic. Utopian idealism is the Left's version. Libertarianism is the Right's. The Left tends to collectivism, the Right to individualism: opposite but connected errors.

7. ANGELISTIC LINGUISTICS

Angels have no bodies, therefore no senses, therefore no imaginations (imagination is the power to conjure up images of sense experiences), therefore no myths and symbols. They are purely intellectual. Their language is as clear and rational as mathematics.

One form of angelistic linguistics, therefore, is the search for one universal "ideal language" that is perfectly clear and unambiguous. Esperanto tries to attain this ideal. It is an artificial language, the simplest and most rational one (and the dullest one) ever invented. Computer language is another artificial language: it translates all meanings into combinations ultimately derived from one and zero.

8. ANGELISTIC LOGIC

Though angels are intuitive rather than logical—they know truth immediately rather than by taking time to move logically step by step from a premise to a conclusion—yet there is an angelistic tendency even in modern logic. This is the replacement of Aristotelian ordinary-language logic with symbolic or mathematical logic—a replacement nearly total in philosophy departments throughout the world. Aristotelian logic begins with concretely meaningful *terms*, like "man" and "apple", whose meanings are learned by (bodily) experience. For example: "All men are rational, and apples are not rational, therefore men are not apples." But symbolic logic abstracts from terms entirely and begins with propositions as its basic units. For example: "If p is true, then q is true. Q is not true. Therefore p is not true." P and q can be any proposition, whether "all men are rational" or "all turtles are gods on Thursday nights". The content of the proposition doesn't matter. In other words, symbolic logic is purely rationalistic and abstracts from all sense experience. Like angels.

Angelism (spiritualism), or immaterialism, and animalism (materialism), though opposites, reinforce each other and swing back and forth like a pendulum, the one reacting to the other. The main reason angelism is so popular in our culture is probably that it is our instinctive reaction against the *materialism* of our culture. Materialism, in turn, is a (natural but exaggerated) reaction against angelism.

Knowing both angels and animals is necessary for knowing ourselves. Pascal says:

"Man must not be allowed to believe that he is equal either to animals or to angels, nor to be unaware of either, but he must know both" (*Pensées* 121).

"Man is neither angel nor beast, and it is unfortunately the case that anyone trying to act the angel acts the beast" (*Pensées* 678).

APPENDIX B
A Snakebite Letter: Sex and the Media

From *The Snakebite Letters* by Peter Kreeft (San Francisco: Ignatius Press, 1994). This is a sample from a series of letters from a senior demon, Snakebite, to an apprentice demon, Braintwister, instructing him in methods of tempting men and winning men's souls from "the Enemy" (God).

My dear Braintwister:

To advise you how best to tempt your patient in matters of sexuality—a vast continent for these disgusting creatures—I need to first give you some background.

Our past success on this front is largely the result of two factors. The two may seem contradictory, yet both work for us. The first is that your patient, like most Americans, is a conformist (though he fancies himself a freethinker). He fears being different, eccentric, or (worst of all) "a fanatic", much more than he fears being wicked. The second factor is that the society to which he aspires to conform is in fact a highly elitist society, dominated by a tiny coterie of opinion molders in the media and educational establishments. This elite is now virtually eating out of our claws. It's generations ahead of the masses in matters of morality and religion.

(We haven't entirely succeeded in dominating their politicians, because Americans elect their representatives—but not their educators or media elite. Yet it's not an insurmountable problem because politicians have far less real power than teachers or magazine writers or moviemakers in current American culture, since they must at least appear to be servants of the people. If they don't reflect popular opinion, they're simply not elected.)

Here are some useful statistics on our media clients. Though nearly half of all Americans attend church at least occasionally, fewer than one in 10 of our elite do. Though 72 percent of

Americans think abortion is somehow bad and should be limited, only 3 percent of our elite do. Though seven out of 10 Americans believe there are moral absolutes, only one in 10 of our elite do. Though eight out of 10 Americans believe in a God they will meet and be judged by after death, only one in 10 in our elite do.

See? We've won the teachers, soon we'll have the students. Once you capture the cause, you soon own the effect. And these teachers aren't limited to the classroom; through TV, movies, magazines and music, we've turned the whole society into a classroom. And the lesson plans are written by us.

We have a right to preen a bit over this success, but we should also be realistic and candid. Not only do we have the usual Enemy counterattacks to fend off, but we're also struggling with a contradiction within our own strategy, and if the humans ever sense it, our plans may be ruined.

Here's the problem. On the one hand, we want the human vermin to be bland, egalitarian conformists. Our strategy has been to produce photocopied souls, and we've labored long and hard (and quite successfully) for more than a century now to rid them of the very concepts of excellence, nobility, superiority, hierarchy and authority. Nearly all of them, when they hear those words, react with a negative knee jerk. Their unconscious creed is: What all cannot attain, no one should.

But on the other hand, the masses remain much more traditional, religious and moral in their beliefs than our elite. (Note the statistics above.) We don't want souls to conform to the real majority just yet—not until the majority is ours. You must therefore keep your patient from noticing the contradiction between his egalitarianism and his elitism.

But here's the good news: You'd be amazed how easy this is. Remember our basic principle of keeping his mind and his morals in separate compartments.

The Enemy wants him to be an elitist about ideas and ideals, and an egalitarian about people; to be suspicious and critical of ideas but open and welcoming to all people. Our strategy is to make him just the opposite: an elitist about people and an egalitarian about ideas. Make him think his teachers and scriptwriters are superior people, but also that one idea isn't really superior to another, that all ideas are equal, that there's no objective truth, no real right and wrong, and thus no one has any right to "impose his own values on others". (You simply will not believe how much mileage we've gotten out of *that* hogwash!)

Once again, keep his mind away from noting the self-contradiction in our propaganda, the value judgment that there are no real value judgments, the dogma against dogma.

How can they not notice such an obvious contradiction? They can, Braintwister, they can—especially the well educated ones. The more educated they are, the less they believe in logic and common sense. It's the farm boys and cleaning women whose minds we've been unable to twist.

Really, did you think the sexual revolution of the 1960s just "happened"? No, it was the flowering of a long, deliberate strategy. The basic principle of our approach is a one-two punch: Hit them where they're soft and weak, and at the same time hit them where they're hard and proud—in other words, between their legs and between their ears.

They've always been soft in the reproductive organs, of course. How typical of the Enemy to invent that obscene joke of a "rational animal", to put an angel-like spirit in an ape-like body! But now we've softened their heads too. They've always had trouble obeying the Enemy's law of chastity; but they've never had such trouble understanding it and believing it until now. It's not new that we've tempted them to live promiscuously, but it's thoroughly novel that we've tempted them to justify it, to glorify it, even to sanctify it.

How did we manage it? We had some success with philosophers, playwrights, artists, novelists and poets over the last century, but our campaign really took off with the advent of movies and TV. The secret is the power of images. The humans can put up defenses against ideas, which have to pass the gate keeper of their mind, Reason; but they're weak as water against images. Images sneak in through their unconscious, which is a helpless child.

If we plant the same kind of image in them over and over again through TV and movies, they'll gradually be desensitized. Sex and violence are our two specialties, of course. Our media elite personnel have relentlessly pressured for more. If the sex and violence curve continues at the current rate, we'll have Hell incarnate in their minds in just two more generations. There's nothing, literally nothing, these creatures won't allow. Already, most things the last generation would have regarded as unthinkable are commonplace on TV.

With the movies, it was a two-step strategy. First, their films showed more explicit sexual promiscuity, but within a moral context—"crime and punishment", so to speak. Movies like *Carnal Knowledge*, *Alfie*, and *Shampoo* typify this stage. Then, once the explicit images became commonplace, the sheep were too passive to protest the removal of the moral frame. Their moralists played right into our strategy; they were so hung up on how much flesh was shown that they forgot the lesson the images taught. They were so shocked at overt eroticism, even in a framework of fidelity, that they hardly noticed the snide little smirks for infidelity.

The upshot is that now, nearly every single movie that's made for young people *must* have a dash of nudity, no matter how gratuitous (and of course never, never between married people). And every time a boy first kisses a girl, the next scene always shows them in bed. What a triumph of image propaganda!

The lesson it bores into them unconsciously, like holes bored in the hull of a ship, is so obvious I'm surprised they don't get bored with it: that the normal, the natural, the inevitable corollary of kissing is copulating.

Notice the power of images, Braintwister. Not even a professor could be fool enough to fall for that as an argument. Put it in words, and it's ridiculous. Put it in images, and it's compelling.

Thus we've persuaded them to rationalize their lust, to believe that feeling, not marriage, justifies sex. Most of them don't yet believe in infidelity, but they do believe in fornication. The only strictures they put on copulating are "emotional maturity" and "commitment", which are vague enough for anyone but an infant to claim.

Oh, we've had a field day with their heads. There have been times and places in the past where we've had as much success with their hormones, but never with their heads. That's because never before has a society been so educated, and never before have we so dominated the education industry, especially the extracurricular one, the media.

We've also succeeded in imposing a total media censorship on the one subject that is the most important thing of all in the lives of the majority of the people in the country, but which is never allowed to enter even the most "realistic" movies or public TV shows. I mean, of course, religious faith. Religion is shown occasionally, but from the outside, and never as *true*. The only characters shown as deeply religious are either bigots or sissies.

Though we've undermined their sexual morality, we haven't yet rotted away the rest of their Christian ethics. We've persuaded only a few to accept cruelty, the last bastion of their moral absolutism; but we've succeeded in glorifying it and desensitizing them to it, for example, just by making "slasher" movies fashionable. Wait till they see the next step!

But we mustn't let our love of violence distract us from our main task. Niceness is as useful as nastiness, stamp collecting is as useful as murder, if only it sucks these vermin from the Enemy's grasp. That's the only thing that matters in the end.

The Enemy has this utterly ridiculous thing about repentance, you know. Sometimes I suspect He deliberately allows us to tempt some of the vermin to great sins just so that they'll see them more clearly and repent more strongly, and thus escape our two most deadly nets, pride and self-satisfaction. That supremely troublesome philosopher Thomas Aquinas let out a secret of the Enemy's strategy when he said that just as a doctor may tolerate a lesser disease to free his patient from a greater one, the Enemy often deliberately withholds that loathsome thing He calls "grace" and allows a soul to succumb to our temptation to some clear, external sin in order to free it from pride and bring it to repentance.

The Enemy really will forgive any sin, you know—that is, any sin He can forgive, i.e., any sin that's repented of. So impenitence is what we must aim at, by dulling their consciences to guilt, making them feel more guilty about guilt than about sin.

Your patient does, unfortunately, have something of a conscience. That's our enemy, Braintwister. Conscience is the Enemy's own mouthpiece in the soul. Shut it down at any cost.

Our end, of course, is not simply to inveigle the brutes into bed with each other, but (1) to win their souls through corrupting their society (after all, a "good" society is simply one where it's easy to be good, as one of their more dangerous but fortunately obscure thinkers, Peter Maurin, has said); (2) to corrupt their society through destroying its fundamental foundation, the family, the one place they naturally learn the Enemy's philosophy of unselfish love, being loved just for who you are, not for what you do; (3) to destroy the family through destroying marriages; (4) to destroy marriages through destroying fidelity, their anchor and glue; (5) to destroy fidelity through the new philosophy of "sexual liberation" and the "sexual revolution"; and (6) to do that through our domination of the media. It's a simple six-step sexual strategy.

One of the most pernicious ideas that can creep into your patient's head is throwing away his TV set. That would burn the bridge by which we march into his heart. But that's an act so radical that few of them are ever capable of it—no junkie likes going cold turkey.

Your affectionate uncle,
Snakebite

"Madonna and Child with Angels" (detail)
S. Apollinare Nuovo, Ravenna, Italy

APPENDIX C
What the New *Catechism of the Catholic Church* Says about Angels

The Existence of Angels—a Truth of Faith

328 The existence of the spiritual, non-corporeal beings that Sacred Scripture usually calls "angels" is a truth of faith. The witness of Scripture is as clear as the unanimity of Tradition.

Who are they?

329 St. Augustine says: "'Angel' is the name of their office, not of their nature. If you seek the name of their nature, it is 'spirit'; if you seek the name of their office, it is 'angel': from what they are, 'spirit,' from what they do, 'angel.'" With their whole beings the angels are *servants* and messengers of God. Because they "always behold the face of my Father who is in heaven" they are the "mighty ones who do his word, hearkening to the voice of his word."

330 As purely *spiritual* creatures angels have intelligence and will: they are personal and immortal creatures, surpassing in perfection all visible creatures, as the splendor of their glory bears witness.

Christ "with all his angels"

331 Christ is the center of the angelic world. They are *his* angels: "When the Son of man comes in his glory, and all the angels with him. . . ." They belong to him because they were created *through* and *for* him: "for in him all things were created in heaven and on earth, visible and invisible, whether thrones or dominions or principalities or authorities—all things were created through him and for him." They belong to him still

From *Catechism of the Catholic Church* (1994).

more because he has made them messengers of his saving plan: "Are they not all ministering spirits sent forth to serve, for the sake of those who are to obtain salvation?"

332 Angels have been present since creation and throughout the history of salvation, announcing this salvation from afar or near and serving the accomplishment of the divine plan: they closed the earthly paradise; protected Lot; saved Hagar and her child; stayed Abraham's hand; communicated the law by their ministry; led the People of God; announced births and callings; and assisted the prophets, just to cite a few examples. Finally, the angel Gabriel announced the birth of the Precursor and that of Jesus himself.

333 From the Incarnation to the Ascension, the life of the Word incarnate is surrounded by the adoration and service of angels. When God "brings the firstborn into the world, he says: 'Let all God's angels worship him.' Their song of praise at the birth of Christ has not ceased resounding in the Church's praise: "Glory to God in the highest!" They protect Jesus in his infancy, serve him in the desert, strengthen him in his agony in the garden, when he could have been saved by them from the hands of his enemies as Israel had been. Again, it is the angels who "evangelize" by proclaiming the Good News of Christ's Incarnation and Resurrection. They will be present at Christ's return, which they will announce, to serve at his judgment.

The angels in the life of the Church

334 In the meantime, the whole life of the Church benefits from the mysterious and powerful help of angels.

335 In her liturgy, the Church joins with the angels to adore the thrice-holy God. She invokes their assistance (in the Roman Canon's *Supplices te rogamus* . . . ["Almighty God, we pray that your angel . . ."]; in the funeral liturgy's *In Paradisum deducant te angeli* . . . ["May the angels lead you into Paradise . . ."]. Moreover, in the "Cherubic Hymn" of the Byzan-

tine Liturgy, she celebrates the memory of certain angels more particularly (St. Michael, St. Gabriel, St. Raphael, and the guardian angels).

336 From infancy to death human life is surrounded by their watchful care and intercession. "Beside each believer stands an angel as protector and shepherd leading him to life." Already here on earth the Christian life shares by faith in the blessed company of angels and men united in God.

The Fall of the Angels

391 Behind the disobedient choice of our first parents lurks a seductive voice, opposed to God, which makes them fall into death out of envy. Scripture and the Church's Tradition see in this being a fallen angel, called "Satan" or the "devil." The Church teaches that Satan was at first a good angel, made by God: "The devil and the other demons were indeed created naturally good by God, but they became evil by their own doing."

392 Scripture speaks of a sin of these angels. This "fall" consists in the free choice of these created spirits, who radically and irrevocably *rejected* God and his reign. We find a reflection of that rebellion in the tempter's words to our first parents: "You will be like God." The devil "has sinned from the beginning"; he is "a liar and the father of lies."

393 It is the *irrevocable* character of their choice, and not a defect in the infinite divine mercy, that makes the angels' sin unforgivable. "There is no repentance for the angels after their fall, just as there is no repentance for men after death."

APPENDIX D

Angels and Demons in the Bible

Listed below is every verse in the Bible mentioning angels and (then) demons, devils, or the Devil. I have found it much more helpful to go through all the Biblical data myself, verse by verse, like a pig with its nose to the ground snuffling for truffles, than to rely on some theological pilot who takes you on a guided tour overhead through carefully selected clouds.

ANGELS

Genesis
- 16:7, 9, 10, 11
- 19:1, 15
- 21:17
- 22:11, 15
- 24:40
- 28:12
- 31:11
- 32:1
- 48:16

Exodus
- 3:2
- 14:19
- 23:20, 23
- 32:34
- 33:2

Numbers
- 20:16
- 22:22, 23, 24, 25, 26, 27, 31, 32, 34, 35

Judges
- 2:1, 4
- 5:23
- 6:11, 12, 20, 21, 22
- 13:3, 6, 9, 13, 15, 16, 17, 18, 19, 20, 21

1 Samuel
- 29:9

2 Samuel
- 14:17, 20
- 19:27
- 24:16, 17

1 Kings
- 13:18
- 19:5, 7

2 Kings
- 1:3, 15
- 19:35

1 Chronicles
- 21:12, 15, 16, 18, 20, 27, 30

2 Chronicles
- 32:21

Job
- 4:18

Psalms
- 8:5
- 34:7
- 35:5, 6
- 68:17
- 78:49
- 91:11
- 103:20
- 104:4
- 148:2

Ecclesiastes
- 5:6

Isaiah
37:36
63:9
Daniel
3:28
6:22
Hosea
12:4
Zechariah
1:9, 11, 12, 13, 14, 19
2:3
3:1, 3, 5, 6
4:1, 4, 5
5:5, 10
6:4, 5
12:8
Matthew
1:20, 24
2:13, 19
4:6, 11
13:39, 41, 49
16:27
18:10
22:30
24:31, 36
25:31, 41
26:53
28:2, 5
Mark
1:13
8:38
12:25
13:27, 32
Luke
1:11, 13, 18, 19, 26, 28, 30, 34, 35, 38
2:9, 10, 13, 15, 21
4:10
9:26
12:8, 9
15:10
16:22
20:36
22:43
24:23
John
1:51
5:4
12:29
20:12
Acts
5:19
6:15
7:30, 35, 38, 53
8:26
10:3, 7, 22
11:13
12:7, 8, 9, 10, 11, 15, 23
23:8, 9
27:23
Romans
8:38
1 Corinthians
4:9
6:3
11:10
13:1
2 Corinthians
11:14
Galatians
1:8
3:19
4:14
Colossians
2:18
2 Thessalonians
1:7
1 Timothy
3:16
5:21
Hebrews
1:4, 5, 6, 7, 13
2:2, 5, 7, 9, 16
12:22
13:2
1 Peter
1:12
3:22

2 Peter
2:4, 11
Jude
6
Revelation
1:1, 20
2:1, 8, 12, 18
3:1, 5, 7, 14
5:2, 11
7:1, 2, 11
8:2, 3, 5, 6, 7, 8, 10, 12, 13, 14, 15
9:14, 15
10:1, 5, 7, 8, 9
11:1, 15
12:7, 9
14:6, 8, 9, 10, 15, 17, 18, 19
15:1, 6, 7, 8
16:1, 3, 4, 5, 8, 10, 12
17:1, 7
18:1, 21
19:17
20:1
21:9, 12, 17
22:6, 8, 16

DEVILS (DEMONS)

Leviticus
17:7
Deuteronomy
32:17
2 Chronicles
11:15
Psalms
106:37
Matthew
4:24
7:22
8:16, 28, 31, 33
9:34
10:8
12:24, 27, 28
Mark
1:32, 24, 29
3:15, 22
5:12
6:13
9:38
16:9, 17
Luke
4:41
8:2, 27, 30, 33, 35, 36, 38
9:1, 49
10:17
11:15, 18, 19, 20
13:32
1 Corinthians
10:20, 21
1 Timothy
4:1
James
2:19
Revelation
9:20
16:14
18:2

EVIL SPIRITS

Leviticus
19:31
20:6
Numbers
16:22
17:16
Deuteronomy
18:11
1 Samuel
28:3, 9
2 Kings
21:6
28:9
Isaiah
8:19
19:3
Matthew
10:1
12:45
Mark
1:27
3:11
5:13
6:7
Luke
4:36
6:18
7:21
8:2
10:20
11:26
Acts
5:16
8:7
19:12, 13
1 Corinthians
12:10
1 Timothy
4:1
1 John
4:1
Revelation
16:13, 14

THE DEVIL

Matthew
4:1, 5, 8, 11
9:32, 33
11:18
12:22
13:39
15:22
17:18
25:41
Mark
5:15, 16, 18
7:26, 29, 30
Luke
4:2, 3, 5, 6, 13, 33, 35
7:33
8:12, 13, 29
9:42
11:14
John
6:70
7:20
8:44, 48, 49, 52
10:20, 21
13:2
Acts
10:38
13:10
Ephesians
4:27
6:11

1 Timothy
3:6, 7
2 Timothy
2:26
Hebrews
2:14
James
4:7
1 Peter
5:8
1 John
3:8, 10
Revelation
2:10
12:9, 12
20:2, 10

SATAN

1 Chronicles
21:1
Job
1:6, 7, 8, 9, 12
2:1, 2, 3, 4, 6, 7
Psalms
109:6
Zechariah
3:1, 2
Matthew
4:10
12:26
16:23
Mark
1:13
3:23, 26
4:15
8:33
Luke
10:18
11:18
13:16
22:3, 31
John
13:37
Acts
5:3
26:18
Romans
16:20
1 Corinthians
5:5
7:5
2 Corinthians
2:11
11:14
12:7
1 Thessalonians
2:18
2 Thessalonians
2:9
1 Timothy
1:20
5:15
Revelation
2:9, 13, 24
3:9
12:9
20:2, 7

BEELZEBUB

Matthew
10:25
12:24, 27

Mark
3:22

Luke
11:15, 18, 19

BIBLIOGRAPHY

Adler, Mortimer. *The Angels and Us*. New York: Macmillan, 1982.

Carroll, Warren H. *Our Lady of Guadalupe and the Conquest of Darkness*. Front Royal, Va.: Christendom College Press, 1983.

Kreeft, Peter. *Everything You Ever Wanted to Know about Heaven But Never Dreamed of Asking*. San Francisco: Ignatius Press, 1983.

———. *Fundamentals of the Faith: Essays in Christian Apologetics*. San Francisco: Ignatius Press, 1988.

———. *The Snakebite Letters*. San Francisco: Ignatius Press, 1994.

Kreeft, Peter, and Ronald K. Tacelli. *Handbook of Christian Apologetics: Hundreds of Answers to Crucial Questions*. Downers Grove, Ill.: Intervarsity Press, 1994.

Lewis, Clive Staples. *Miracles*. New York: Collier Macmillan, 1947, 1960.

———. *Out of the Silent Planet*. New York: Collier Macmillan, 1952, 1965.

———. *Perelandra*. New York: Collier, 1944.

———. *That Hideous Strength*. New York: Collier Macmillan, 1946.

Montgomery, John Warwick, *Principalities and Powers*. Minneapolis: Bethany House, 1991.

Tolkien, J. R. R. *The Silmarillion*. New York: Houghton-Mifflin, 1977; Ballantine Books, 1985.

ART CREDITS

Page	Source
2	Art Resource, New York Doré, Gustav. *Illustration to Old Testament*: "The Angel Appearing to Joshua".
16	Giraudon/Art Resource, New York Doré, Gustav. *History of the Crusades by Michaud*: "The Night of August 25, 1270, the Death of St. Louis". Bibliothèque Nationale, Paris, France.
26	Giraudon/Art Resource, New York Abraham's sacrifice. Psalter of Ingeburg of Denmark (Ms. 9/1695), folio 11. France, 13th century. Musée Condé, Chantilly, France.
34	Scala/Art Resource, New York Icon with depiction of Annunciation. 16th century. National Museum, Belgrade, Yugoslavia.
40	Scala/Art Resource, New York Raphael. *St. Peter Freed from Prison by the Angel.* Stanze de Raffaello (detail). Vatican Palace, Vatican State.
46	Scala/Art Resource, New York *Celestial Hierarchy* (detail with angels). Duomo, Cefalu, Italy.
64	Scala/Art Resource, New York Gozzoli, Benozzo. *Angels in Adoration* (detail of an angel). Palazzo Medici Riccardi, Florence, Italy.
99	Erich Lessing/Art Resource, New York Detail of an angel, mosaic. S. Apollinare in Classe, Ravenna, Italy. S. Apollinare Nuovo, Ravenna, Italy.
110	Bridgeman/Art Resource, New York *God Testing Job's Faith by Allowing the Devil to Destroy Job's Sheep.* Ms. Latin 15675. Bibliothèque Nationale, Paris, France.
117	Giraudon/Art Resource, New York Limbourg Brothers, *Très Riches Heures du Duc de Berry*: "Fall of the Rebel Angels". 15th century. Musée Condé, Chantilly, France.
144	Scala/Art Resource, New York *Madonna Enthroned with Four Angels* (detail). S. Apollinare Nuovo, Ravenna, Italy.